"A nuanced and yet accessible introduction to the fascinating world of cybersecurity. Stevens brings a refreshingly critical eye to some of its main challenges and practices, clearly showing how cybersecurity is fundamentally political."
André Barrinha, University of Bath

"Insightfully acknowledging that cybersecurity is social and political, Stevens offers a comprehensive but still succinct overview that is a valuable resource to anyone interested in learning how cybersecurity challenges have emerged, how different forms of security come at the expense of each other and how actors address their insecurities."
Amir Lupovici, Tel Aviv University

"A great book to engage with the security implications of a rapidly digitalizing world beyond the technical. Heed its central message: cybersecurity is about and for humans!"
**Myriam Dunn Cavelty,
Center for Security Studies, ETH Zürich**

"By far the clearest and most insightful reflection on the purpose of cybersecurity policies and activities, their evolution, their failures and successes that I have recently had the pleasure of reading. It tells you that cybersecurity is not, and never was, a fringe field of technical security, but rather a key guarantor of our way of life. Accessible to a wider audience, the book makes a fundamental contribution to society's understanding of why we should all strive to learn more about cybersecurity."
Helena Farrand Carrapico,
Northumbria University

"A long overdue look at the human and political dimensions of cybersecurity, this book covers a lot of ground with real insight, vision and intelligence."
Madeline Carr, University College London

"An excellent primer on cybersecurity, with an emphasis on the often overlooked human and political dimensions. An essential resource."
Ron Deibert, University of Toronto

The status quo is broken. Humanity today faces multiple interconnected challenges, some of which could prove existential. If we believe the world could be different, if we want it to be *better*, examining the purpose of what we do – and what is done in our name – is more pressing than ever.

The What Is It For? series examines the purpose of the most important aspects of our contemporary world, from religion and free speech to animal rights and the Olympics. It illuminates what these things are by looking closely at what they do.

The series offers fresh thinking on current debates that gets beyond the overheated polemics and easy polarizations. Across the series, leading experts explore new ways forward, enabling readers to engage with the possibility of real change.

Series editor: George Miller

Visit **bristoluniversitypress.co.uk/whats-it-for** to find out more about the series.

TIM STEVENS is Reader in International Security at the Department of War Studies, King's College London, and director of the King's Cyber Security Research Group. He has published widely on the politics of cybersecurity, cyberwarfare and cyber conflict, and the relationship between technology and global security. He is the author or editor of four books and the editor of the book series, Critical Issues in Digital Security and Society.

WHAT IS CYBERSECURITY FOR?

TIM STEVENS

First published in Great Britain in 2023 by

Bristol University Press
University of Bristol
1–9 Old Park Hill
Bristol
BS2 8BB
UK
t: +44 (0)117 374 6645
e: bup-info@bristol.ac.uk

Details of international sales and distribution partners are available at
bristoluniversitypress.co.uk

British Library Cataloguing in Publication Data
A catalogue record for this book is available from the British Library

ISBN 978-1-5292-2695-9 paperback
ISBN 978-1-5292-2696-6 ePub
ISBN 978-1-5292-2697-3 ePdf

Cover design: Tom Appshaw
Bristol University Press uses environmentally
responsible print partners.
Printed and bound in Great Britain by
TJ Books, Padstow

CONTENTS

LIST OF FIGURES AND TABLES

Figures

Tables

1
INTRODUCTION: A 'WICKED PROBLEM'

'Oops, your files have been encrypted!' This message greeted staff of the UK's National Health Service (NHS) when they tried to access their computers and other digital devices on 12 May 2017. The screen that popped up informed them that their data had been encoded in such a way that to restore it they would have to pay a $300 ransom in something called Bitcoin or risk losing it forever. Worse, all the computer systems affected – including a significant percentage of primary healthcare providers like hospitals and doctors' surgeries – would cease to function in the meantime, leaving frontline and support staff unable to treat their patients, book appointments, or conduct business reliant on NHS digital services. At 4 pm the NHS declared a major incident and switched to backup systems wherever possible. It also disconnected uninfected networks as a precaution, with knock-on effects on service provision even where the malicious software (malware) that became known as WannaCry had not been detected. Within a few hours, the one British institution that for decades had enjoyed very high levels of public trust started to wonder if it could fulfil its statutory duties as the public healthcare provider of first resort to nearly seventy million people. As the media went into overdrive, the government scrambled to resolve what looked like a knock-out blow to the NHS and its millions of users.

Fortunately, a researcher analysing the WannaCry code found in it a 'kill switch': once activated, this prevented further infection and gave security professionals the time needed to deploy defensive measures. By that evening, the spread of WannaCry across the NHS was halted and the job began of cleaning up its networks and implementing measures that, as subsequent investigations found, should already have been in place.[1] Over the next few weeks it became clear that, while British attention was understandably focused on the NHS, it was only one of thousands of organizations that had been affected in over 150 countries, with some estimating global economic losses of up to $4 billion.[2] WannaCry continues to wander across the world's digital networks and, even though no one died as a direct result of its disruption to the NHS, the potential for harm to life and livelihoods from errant computer code was amply demonstrated to many people for the first time.

WannaCry was a very public lapse in cybersecurity. If we think of cybersecurity first as the protection of computer networks and systems from uninvited compromise and damage, this incident saw the insertion of malware into digital environments that prevented them functioning as intended by their designers and users. Good cybersecurity could have prevented rampant infection by WannaCry: if organizations had maintained their systems by updating the Microsoft Windows software targeted by WannaCry, the malware could not have entered as it did. In the language of cybersecurity, WannaCry exploited an unpatched vulnerability in versions of the Windows operating system. Patching that vulnerability would have prevented the worst of the damage and saved a great deal of public and political concern. At least in theory. As this book will explain, cybersecurity is a necessary but imperfect aspect of the contemporary world. It can never be absolute, and nor perhaps should we wish that it were: 'total security' is the ambition of despots, not democracies. Bad things will happen in the networks, and we should learn how to prepare for them and how to do things better in the future.

The story of cybersecurity is interwoven with the digital transformation of the modern world. Few of us are not touched profoundly by the information technologies of the cellphone and the Internet, of smart homes and smart cities, of new ways of conducting business and connecting to one another through the Internet and other digital technologies. If, as some claim, this is a truly revolutionary stage of human development, it hinges on the creation, exchange and exploitation of information. Digital ones and zeroes pass across continents and oceans at vast speeds, through a staggeringly complicated array of hardware and software to which most of us give little thought. We have built the most complex technical system ever devised, one that underpins almost everything we do as individuals, communities and societies. This intensive process of information-technological development has transformed how we work, learn and live, how we create economic value and foster political engagement, how we deliver critical services from energy to healthcare, and the ways in which countries pursue their national interests through conflict and competition. A world in which the Internet does not play a fundamental role is almost unimaginable: it seems an essential fact of life.

Building something as large and complex as the Internet raises an important consideration: how do we maintain it so that we continue to enjoy its benefits? If we design something properly, it should mostly run as intended, without the need for frequent maintenance and repair. When things do break, we should be able to fix them rapidly and without disrupting the services on which we depend. In the case of digital transformation, however, in our enthusiasm for rolling out global digital infrastructures and the billions of devices and applications that run on them, we have created a problem. This problem is threefold. The first problem is that our dependence on information technologies is itself a source of vulnerability. If something goes wrong with a business software system, a banking application or digital healthcare provision, those services potentially become unavailable to those who need them, with multiple knock-on effects. Switching back to older, analogue ways of doing things might not be enough, if it is even possible. The second problem is that, for a variety of historical reasons, the Internet and almost everything reliant on it are prone to errors of design, implementation and use. Systems are set up incorrectly, software configured badly and users make mistakes. Data is lost, services go down, and people and businesses suffer. It is very difficult – perhaps even mathematically impossible – to design a digital system entirely free of these issues.

The third problem is intimately related to the first two: enough people understand these vulnerabilities and seek to exploit them that cyberspace – the notional environment in which our digital interactions take place – has become a magnet for diverse actors who threaten both its integrity and our ability to engage in legitimate Internet-dependent activities. As we move business online, we inadvertently provide opportunities for criminals to steal, defraud and extort through innovative digital means. Vast datasets created by companies and countries form targets for new types of digital intelligence and espionage. Those datasets are the product of corporate and national surveillance, and the information-gathering devices which populate our homes, offices and streets in their billions. National militaries and intelligence agencies conduct cyberwarfare operations against one another in peace and war, to the extent that cyberwarfare may have become a defining feature of a persistent state of competition somewhere between the two. The countries engaged in this competition disagree about what should and should not be allowed in global cyberspace, a diplomatic discussion plagued by geopolitical contestation and the pursuit of strategic advantage. All these activities are enabled by the deliberate exploitation of technical vulnerabilities in digital systems and by the manipulation and deception of end-users like you and me.

This is the world of cybersecurity and the subject of this book. The ostensible purpose of cybersecurity is to protect computer networks and systems from compromise and damage. In its classical form, when it was usually known as 'information security', the aim was to secure computing resources and ensure the confidentiality, integrity and availability of data for legitimate users. This is still a primary goal of cybersecurity, undertaken round the clock by millions of highly skilled technicians and administrators. Their task is to keep things running, often under serious challenge from cybercriminals, hackers, spies, militaries and adventurers. In a technical sense, then, cybersecurity is a distinct form of security: it secures computer networks and systems and the data stored in or in transit across them. Despite cybersecurity professionals' remarkable work, the fundamental problems outlined above persist. We have not yet seen a large-scale collapse of the global Internet, but we have experienced many outages and breakdowns that have affected parts of it, as well as countless lower-level incidents, each of which has social and economic costs. This implies something even more fundamental about cybersecurity.

All forms of security exist to secure something. This may seem obvious, but it has important implications for how we think about cybersecurity, as this book will explore. The purpose of national security is to secure the nation, to protect it from external and internal threats and preserve its political sovereignty and territorial integrity. When we think of international security, we understand it mainly as states cooperating to enable their peaceful coexistence. Nuclear security, environmental security, economic security, energy security – they all secure a distinct resource, or people's access to that resource. We can argue about whether 'security' is the appropriate term to use in respect of, for example, the environment, but this does not alter its common use in politics and policy. This is also the case for cybersecurity, which is a staple of contemporary public policy. Countries develop cybersecurity policies and strategies, as do international forums like the United Nations, European Union and the G7. Those documents, however, are not principally about technical issues. They treat cybersecurity not just as the security of computer networks and systems, although that is a key ambition, but as a way of achieving other forms of security too. Cybersecurity provides security to a range of 'referents', as security studies scholars call the entities to which a particular form of security refers. It is no longer, if it ever was, just about technical security: it is essential to higher-level forms of security, like national and international security, and of guaranteeing continuity in people's everyday lives, as suggested by the term, 'human security', discussed later in this book. These concerns are underwritten by the growing awareness that cyber operations can have significant effects in the physical world. Had WannaCry not been stopped so quickly, we could have seen that 'cyber-physical' scenario play out in human casualties and deaths.

This makes cybersecurity a difficult analytical and practical problem. It may even be a 'wicked problem', a term that emerged in the 1960s to describe problems that were difficult not only to solve but even to define. This resonates when we think about the problem – or problems – of cybersecurity: which problem are we seeking to address and, as the wicked problem concept additionally suggests, can we be certain our proposed solution will not make things worse, since wicked problems always intersect with other problem sets? If our 'solution' to the 'problem' of nuclear weapons is to abolish them, can we guarantee this will not lead to increased conventional war between major powers? No, we cannot, so we must proceed cautiously in moving towards a nuclear weapons-free world. Something similar applies to cybersecurity: its complexity means that we might inadvertently prioritize one form of security over another, such as national security at the expense of human security. We will return to this problem at the end of this book. This book cannot 'solve' cybersecurity, but it will outline issues of tension and contention in the broad field of cybersecurity. It will also, I hope, provide tools for thinking about cybersecurity. These will be developed throughout the book and revolve around three principal insights or propositions.

The first proposition concerns the relationship between people and technology. Technology is not divorced from the people who design or use it. We are all in a relationship with technologies, with which we interact in mutual and interesting ways. Humans design technologies; they make decisions about what technologies should do and what rules they should follow. We embed values in technology and express those values through it, values that others contest and subvert. The designers of social media platforms, for instance, assume that people sharing personal information has positive value and design their technologies accordingly. Others, including governments, may see in those same technologies insidious threats emerging from the relatively unfettered exchange of information. Technologies also shape our own behaviours, as they allow or encourage certain actions but not others. When we think of cybersecurity, we need to consider its sociotechnical nature, in which humans and nonhumans interrelate in complex fashion. Cybersecurity solutions cannot always be universal, as sociotechnical contexts vary from place to place and from time to time.

The second insight extends the first. Cybersecurity is about human behaviours and ambitions, as well as the technical workings of hardware and software, so we cannot view it as a purely technical problem. This is not to diminish the role of computer scientists or cybersecurity professionals; we need skilled people to address the myriad technical issues that emerge in complex IT systems. However, those systems are sociotechnical and are used and abused for human ends. You cannot address issues of cybercriminality or cyberwarfare through technical means alone, nor develop cybersecurity law, policy and regulation without reference to non-technological frameworks and ideas. Scientists and technologists are key allies but, if cybersecurity is a wicked problem, it cannot be defined in wholly scientific terms and so cannot be resolved through science alone. Cybersecurity needs to be understood and addressed from multiple perspectives, drawn from social science, law, philosophy, ethics, psychology and elsewhere, and also from civil society and the public realm.

The third proposition is that cybersecurity is political. This might sound an odd claim, given cybersecurity's preoccupation with computers and code, which seem a world away from 'normal' politics. As I hope to show, how we have built the contemporary world means we cannot but think of cybersecurity as political. It is entangled with almost everything we do, from online shopping, social media, finance, work, play and voting to critical infrastructures supporting every personal and social need, to war, conflict, development and visions of global order. It is also political because this importance is recognized in public policy and resources are allocated to it. It is political because what cybersecurity does or does not do has profound implications for states and citizens everywhere: without cybersecurity, there is no digital transformation worth the name. Politics also implies the possibility of change: cybersecurity might be different in the future.

This book adopts a less technical approach than some readers may expect or desire. I do not assume that you already know how computers or the Internet work; that won't be necessary to engage with the ideas and examples that follow. The jargon of cybersecurity discourages many people from engaging with it, which is deeply unfortunate: this is precisely the time when it needs to be addressed most urgently and, to repurpose a phrase from a classic work of information security, 'given enough eyeballs, all bugs are shallow'.[3] Those eyeballs cannot belong only to technologists, because those bugs are not just technical: they are social, economic and political too. It follows that cybersecurity workforces must also be diverse and inclusive in order to better represent the make-up and interests of the societies they aim to serve.[4]

The book is structured as follows. Chapter 2, 'How Did We Get Here?', provides an overview of how cybersecurity emerged, first as a technical concern and then as a matter of public interest and policy. The Internet was designed for simplicity, not security, a decision whose consequences shape the global information environment today. The chapter relates the changing relationship between computers and security to illustrate how we became dependent on information technologies and explains the key dynamics that have given rise to cybersecurity as a way of managing cyber risks and threats. This provides a springboard to discussing four 'problem sets', addressed in the four subsequent chapters.

Chapter 3, 'Cybersecurity, Cyber Risk', describes the cyber threat landscape in more detail, particularly the distinction between criminal and political cyber threats. It looks at what is threatened by them, which allows us to explore what cybersecurity means to secure. This reveals that cybersecurity has many different and sometimes competing objectives. This chapter also offers a provisional definition of cybersecurity and outlines how cyber risk management and cyber resilience have evolved as complementary modes of coping with the problems of cyber insecurity.

Chapter 4, 'States and Markets', explains how cybersecurity is bound up with the actions and ambitions of states and the private sector. The private sector owns and operates most digital infrastructure for profit; governments seek to regulate and exploit these environments, both for the public good and in the national interest. This chapter looks at how private and public sectors work together to improve cybersecurity and some of the problems that arise when they do. It also explores some of the other difficulties in aligning political and corporate motives, and their impact on cybersecurity.

Chapter 5, 'International Cybersecurity', is about global cyberspace as a competitive domain. It looks at how states attempt to achieve their objectives through offensive cybersecurity, foreign policy and diplomacy. It discusses global governance as a way of collectively addressing cybersecurity and problems of international security and stability, and the ways in which states contest fundamental notions of cyber norms, law and sovereignty. This chapter underscores that cybersecurity is a matter of geopolitics and therefore highly consequential to international order.

Chapter 6, 'Cybersecurity and Human Security', proposes that we should view cybersecurity from the perspective of human security, which attempts to ensure individuals' freedom from fear and want. This shifts the emphasis of cybersecurity significantly and away from national security in particular. The chapter looks at how this changes our notions of cyber risk, state–citizen relations and international cybersecurity, illustrated with examples drawn from digital surveillance and cyberwarfare. Chapter 7 concludes the volume by reaffirming the commitment to human security as a central organizing principle of cybersecurity and addresses the question, 'what is cybersecurity for?'

2
HOW DID WE GET HERE?

This book contends that cybersecurity is central to understanding our contemporary technological condition. It is both a response to the landscape of cyber threats (described in detail in Chapter 3) and a means of securing global digital transformation in its social, economic and political aspects, given their dependence on the proper functioning of the Internet and other digital networks. But why are we even talking about 'cyber' security? The word 'cyber' derives from various Greek words that revolve around the notion of governance or steering, and first came to prominence in the new sciences of cybernetics in the 1940s and 1950s. One of the leading lights of cybernetics described it as 'control and communication in the animal and the machine',[1] which implies a capacity to govern human and nonhuman systems by complex interactions of inputs and outputs. Given that computers work by processing inputs into outputs, it is perhaps unsurprising that 'cyber' was borrowed from the 1980s onwards to describe the novel environments enabled by computers (cyberspace) and for diverse forms of associated activity, from cybersex to cyberculture. We shall encounter several such terms in this book, like cybercrime and cyberwarfare and, of course, cybersecurity, none of which was in common usage before the 2000s. Cybersecurity affirms the link between computers and security, but it is not just about the information security of computers or data, as the brief historical review in this chapter will demonstrate.

To make this argument requires that we understand the evolution of networked computing in wider terms than its scientific and technical development alone. All technologies are situated in specific social, economic and political contexts: society and technology shape one another in profound and sometimes unexpected ways, and these dynamics shift and change over time. This is certainly the case for digital computing technologies, which, from their academic origins in the 1930s, became rapidly entangled with politics, war, economics and society at large. Computers have long been important to national security, for instance, a crucial relationship that is central to cybersecurity now in a way that the term 'information security' does not capture fully. This chapter explains how we have arrived at a point where cybersecurity is the focus of national and international attention, such is its importance to modern societies. The chapter looks at the relationship between computers and security through four lenses.

The first, 'Computers', relates the emergence of modern computers and their relationship with war and national security. It then looks at the early formulations of information security, the tenets and warnings of which remain foundations of cybersecurity today. 'Networks' describes how computing technologies were interconnected in the 1960s through a set of basic technologies, thereby providing the foundation for the modern Internet. This was also when the first hackers emerged, and new computer viruses and worms began to circulate. 'Globalization' of information technologies in the 1980s and 1990s, and the development of the World Wide Web, saw enormous growth in social and economic uses of the Internet, as well as new forms of digital espionage, warfare and crime. By the 2000s, we begin to think of these technologies as 'Infrastructure', through which we reframe digital insecurity as something of societal, perhaps even systemic, importance. Taken together, this is the back story of modern cybersecurity, the present contours of which we will look at in more depth in subsequent chapters.

Computers

From the eighteenth century, people employed as scientific number-crunchers – in tasks such as generating practical information for astronomical and nautical almanacs – were commonly referred to as 'computers', a usage that persisted in some places until the 1950s.[2] Our modern understanding of computers as calculating machines emerged in the nineteenth century through the work of pioneers such as Ada Lovelace and Charles

Babbage.[3] Although it was never built – a modern reconstruction can be seen in London's Science Museum – Babbage's Analytical Engine established modern computing by conceptualizing a machine that could be programmed time and again to convert data, fed into it on cardboard punch cards, into a range of outputs specific to the task at hand, such as producing tables of logarithms and other mathematical functions. Unlike modern computers, this would have been a strictly mechanical affair, with finely engineered cogs and wheels performing calculations that today are undertaken by integrated circuits (microchips). It was only later that the exchange of electrical information via switches and relays was used successfully in programmable electromechanical computers, such as those built by Konrad Zuse in Germany in the early 1940s.

Computing historians argue about the details of invention timelines, but the Atanasoff-Berry Computer (ABC) of 1942, which used electronic vacuum tubes, is widely regarded as the first 'automatic electronic digital computer'. At around the same time, the famous codebreakers of Bletchley Park built Colossus in 1943–4, the first fully programmable electronic digital computer. These were digital rather than analogue machines because the signals (data) used by them were stored and transmitted as either on or off, rather than as constant streams of signals of varying values. Humans take in signals from their environment in continuous analogue fashion, hence an infinite variety of experience of sounds and colours. Digital devices code the same inputs as discontinuous ones (on) and zeroes (off), which allows for easier storage and processing. All digital computing relies on on/off – binary – choices, very commonly of the IF/THEN variety: IF this condition applies, THEN make this happen. These decision-making processes are programs or algorithms, the first theories of which were set out in the 1930s by Alonzo Church and Alan Turing, who essentially invented computer science.

The political context of the Second World War is important to the history of computing. Zuse's first machines were not funded by the German military but soon attracted their attention. Turing's pre-war forays into computing theory saw him drafted into the British cryptographic war effort. The United States' first properly programmable digital computer, the ENIAC, was only finished at the end of the war but was put to work immediately in thermonuclear weapons research. Military applications and funding continued to be critical to computing during the Cold War. In this early period, computers were considered essential tools for furthering national security objectives, rather than as things that needed to be secured. As transistors replaced vacuum tubes and computing efficiency skyrocketed after the war, private firms like IBM began to manufacture computers for specialist business and academic use.[4] Hardware (physical computers and related devices) were distinguished from software, the programs that ran the applications and services on the hardware and the proliferating languages they were written in. Security concerns were mainly restricted to how to prevent illicit physical access to what were huge installations, often occupying whole rooms in companies and universities. As more terminals were deployed on work and study campuses to link remote users to these central computing facilities at the same time ('time-sharing'), these concerns shifted, as non-expert users became connected to one another. It became apparent that some could access and modify data held in centralized repositories, a realization that grew alongside the first formalizations of modern information security.

One of the foundational texts of information security is a 1970 report sponsored by the US Department of Defense and led by computer scientist Willis H. Ware.[5] Ware and his team set out a comprehensive list of security problems that any cybersecurity professional would recognize today. Their central argument was that there were technical solutions to the problems of 'external attack, accidental disclosure, internal subversion, and denial of use to legitimate users', but only for systems that were tightly controlled in classified workspaces, as in government and military installations. Anything more 'open', like the interconnected, multi-user computer environments then burgeoning across the rich countries of Europe, Japan and North America (see Figure 1), was demonstrably insecure and no technological fixes then existed. Moreover, it insisted on the importance of design from the ground up, so that a 'combination of hardware, software, communication, physical, personnel, and administrative-procedural safeguards is required for comprehensive security.'[6]

Figure 1: Computer network vulnerabilities as conceptualized in the Ware Report (1970)

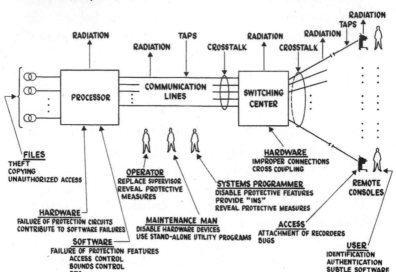

By the mid-1970s, the so-called CIA triad (see Figure 2) had been widely adopted as the core of information security in the digital age. It had always been necessary to protect the confidentiality, integrity and availability of communications, as the long history of code-making and -breaking attests, but the new digital information systems of this period called for an urgent rethink of these requirements. Confidentiality aimed to protect data from unauthorized access. Integrity would ensure data were not tampered with in storage, use or transit. Availability required that data should be available when needed by a legitimate end-user. Achieving these goals is a 'team sport', as the Ware Report indicated, involving

Figure 2: The CIA triad

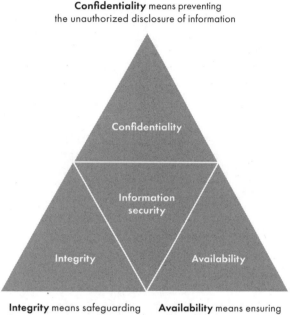

Confidentiality means preventing
the unauthorized disclosure of information

Integrity means safeguarding
the completeness and accuracy
of information and
information processing

Availability means ensuring
that authorized users have
access to information
when they need it

alignment of effort by a range of professionals, some
explicitly technological, others more involved with
process and policy, or training and the development
of organizational 'security cultures'. These principles
and practices have been challenged and augmented for
decades but remain central to information security and
cybersecurity. Implementing security controls informed
by the CIA triad will not guarantee security, but it will
help significantly. Even the most up-to-date national
cybersecurity policies, for instance, continue to make

direct reference to the CIA triad and its essential place in contemporary cybersecurity.[7]

Networks

The CIA triad was to come under intense focus as digital networking expanded and intensified. When we consider digital networks, we usually think of the Internet, which is more accurately described as a network of networks that operate according to shared rules and protocols. By the time the Ware Report was published in 1970, the US and UK were already experimenting with early versions of what would become the Internet. Through the mid- to late 1960s, the US Department of Defense's Advanced Research Projects Agency (ARPA) funded research into large-scale 'internetworking' of universities and government research centres to facilitate data sharing and collaboration. In contrast to existing resource-sharing networks, which tended to collapse if one or more nodes or communication lines were faulty or became disconnected, the so-called ARPANET would break data traffic into small 'packets', stamp them with digital 'to' and 'from' addresses, and send them via the most efficient available routes to their intended destinations. The technology enabling this was invented independently in both the US and UK and became known as 'packet switching'. As if to further illustrate the connection between computers and national security, the US creator of packet switching, Paul Baran, had for years researched how to design military communications systems that could survive a nuclear attack and thereby enable US nuclear retaliation.[8] Contrary to popular myth, the ARPANET was not itself designed to withstand nuclear war but the underlying packet-switching protocols were.

The ARPANET became operational in 1969, linking universities on the West Coast and then military and research establishments across the continental United States. The first international connections were established by satellite to the UK and Norway in 1973. More packet-switching networks, distinct from the ARPANET, emerged in the years that followed. To overcome differences between how these local networks were designed and operated, US researchers developed what remain the core protocols – agreed sets of rules – for how individual networks should connect to the growing ARPANET. What became known as TCP/IP (Transmission Control Protocol/Internet Protocol) allowed for true 'internetworking' of distant networks: as long as a local network used TCP/IP it could connect to the ARPANET and then to users anywhere in the world.[9] Two design decisions are important for understanding this development and its relevance to cybersecurity. The first, in contrast to the closed military origins of the ARPANET, was a presumption to openness: open-architecture networking. These protocols were designed for relatively unfettered exchange of data, something that the Ware Report had warned would be difficult to secure. The second is the end-to-end principle of networking. The end nodes of the network, operated by firms, universities and government agencies, were responsible for security and reliability, not the network itself. The network was a means of providing access to global information space, rather than controlling who or what was connected to it. The ARPANET infrastructure was, in a sense, neutral; it would be users who made decisions about security.

The set of users connecting to the network grew rapidly in the 1980s, as innovative companies marketed microcomputers for home and small business users, powered by ever-smaller and cheaper microprocessors. I recall using a ZX Spectrum 48k at home in the early 1980s, which was not connected to the outside world but could have used a modem and a fixed telephone line to do so. Businesses, researchers and hobbyists did use modems to communicate with suppliers, clients and the like-minded, taking the first steps towards what we would today recognize as a truly global information network of opportunity and economic growth. Many microcomputer users adopted electronic mail (email), which had been around since the early 1970s, and in the 1980s occupied increasing percentages of global bandwidth, including the rapidly growing problem of unsolicited bulk emails (spam).[10] The first commercial Internet service providers emerged in the late 1980s; some bundled proprietary email services with their subscription packages, a visionary move given that there were still fewer than a million users of the emerging Internet worldwide at this point.

The early days of networking were also a testing ground for hackers. This term originally referred to people who enjoyed pushing the boundaries of what these exciting new devices could do. There were many such enthusiasts in the communities that invented the ARPANET and everything that followed. This positive connotation gave way in the 1980s to today's use of 'hacker' to describe someone deliberately undermining computer and network security.[11] The first computer viruses and worms were developed by hackers during this period and began to attract public attention.[12] Viruses are software that attach themselves to files and programs, like spam email, and spread through systems and networks as those files and programs are activated and distributed. Worms are similar but do not require a host file to be activated: once inside, these stand-alone programs propagate themselves. Each exploits bugs and vulnerabilities and each has the potential to cause significant damage by corrupting files, degrading performance or providing bridgeheads for more disruptive software to enter. An experimental virus, Creeper, spread across the ARPANET in the early 1970s, and its programmer later produced a worm version too. It caused no damage as such, displaying the message, 'I'm the Creeper; catch me if you can', but others were less benign. The Morris Worm (1988) was not meant to cause damage but ended up 'bricking' (making unusable) thousands of computers connected to the Internet. It also resulted in the first prosecution under new US computer misuse legislation and prompted the US government to establish the first computer emergency response team (CERT) to coordinate responses to future network crises.[13] The 1980s also saw the first antivirus vendors take to the market and offer software to protect end-users from these new forms of insecurity.

Globalization

The years either side of 1990 were a watershed in modern history, as the Soviet Union collapsed and the Cold War ended. They are notable too in the history of the Internet and its implications for security. In keeping with the global deregulation of telecommunications markets at the time, the US government relinquished control of the nascent Internet, and network access was provided by commercial entities competing for profit. In 1991, the World Wide Web was released, accessible through a web browser, which together may claim to be one of the most important technologies ever developed. 'The Web' is a software application that sits on top of the Internet and allows users to access individually tagged digital resources – files, photos, webpages, videos, software, goods, services – via hyperlinks that are stable over time. The twin dynamics of commercialization and increased accessibility via the Web spurred rapid and highly consequential growth. Not only was the Internet a demonstrable effect of the opening-up and interconnection of economies on a global scale after the Cold War – often referred to as a modern globalization, spurred by capitalism and neoliberalism – but it was a driver of that globalization too. The Internet has encouraged unprecedented forms of social and economic interaction, transnational political mobilization, international cooperation, scientific exchange and technological innovation, bringing distant societies and economies into deeper mutual contact than before. It has also, as any observer of cybersecurity will attest, enabled new forms of mischief and disruption through the Internet, some of which challenge national security and prosperity.

By 1986 hackers working for the KGB were found to have compromised military and industrial computer systems in the West and the contours of networked computer espionage began to come into focus.[14] In the mid- to late 1990s a cyberespionage operation thought to be connected to the Russian government extracted large volumes of classified data from US government agencies, including NASA, the Department of Defense and the Department of Energy.[15] So concerned was the US government by these breaches and their apparent inability to defend against them that it ran a classified exercise called Eligible Receiver in 1997. Posing as an enemy 'red team', National Security Agency (NSA) operators managed, with relative ease, to gain access to three dozen government networks, including military command-and-control systems, intelligence agencies and much else.[16] Whatever lessons might have been learned from this chastening experience, it did not stop the Chinese, with hackers from the People's Liberation Army targeting US and UK defence-industrial and government organizations in the early 2000s in an operation that became known as 'Titan Rain'.[17]

The Internet was facilitating cyberespionage at distance; states no longer needed to insert human agents into each other's territories to gather intelligence. It was different, too, from traditional signals intelligence, in which spies would listen in on enemy communications to collect information. These passive operations were giving way to the possibility of more active interventions by states in the computer networks of their adversaries, in which conventional distinctions between military and intelligence operations became blurred. Cyberwarfare was touted as the next revolutionary development in international affairs, with suitably equipped government agencies able to reach into foreign government networks and cause disruption and damage, in peacetime and in war. The global distribution of cyber capabilities and knowledge was also drawing new actors into this emerging space of conflict.

During Eligible Receiver, the NSA red team had used 'open source' software, freely available to anyone with the knowledge and resolve to do so. When the Chinese embassy in Belgrade was bombed by US aircraft in 1999 during Operation Allied Force, Chinese hackers responded by defacing US government websites, forcing them offline. The situation escalated, as hackers supporting NATO retaliated in kind against China, ushering in a form of cyber conflict between civilians on both sides.[18] Hostilities between hacker groups also flared up after a US reconnaissance plane collided with a Chinese fighter jet over the South China Sea in 2001.[19] Politically motivated hacking – hacktivism – also emerged. In 1998, the hacker group Milw0rm breached the systems of an Indian nuclear research facility in protest at India's nuclear weapons programme, erasing and stealing sensitive data and leaving a public message – 'Don't think destruction is cool, cuz it's not' – on the institution's website.[20] Later that year, American hacktivists tampered with Chinese Internet filtering systems to draw attention to digital human rights abuses in China.[21]

Cyberespionage, hacktivism and digital conflict grabbed the headlines, but it was cybercrime that benefited most from the globalization of the Internet and continues to be the principal scourge of cybersecurity. An Internet with staggering growth rates in the 1990s was always going to attract the attention of criminals and chancers looking to exploit firms and consumers. Analysts often talk of the network effects of the Internet, by which they mean the value of a network to its users increases as more people connect to it. Economists attend to economies of scale, whereby the new digital products and services of the Internet could be produced ever more cheaply per unit as more people joined it. These twin dynamics fuelled the extraordinary growth in e-commerce during this period – and the dot-com boom and bust of the early 2000s, when investor speculation outstripped realistic economic returns – but could be leveraged by criminals too. Cyber legislation and law enforcement were weak, which further emboldened miscreants, some motivated by the old hacker ethos of playing and tinkering but others by the promise of profit. Website defacements were one thing, or even sending annoying email spam – 'Global Alert for All: Jesus is Coming Soon', being one infamous large-scale spam in 1994 – but deliberate attempts to hack into financial systems were another. The 1994 extraction of $10 million from Citibank's electronic transfer system is widely regarded as the harbinger of future cybercrime, an event described by the US Federal Bureau of Investigation as 'bank robbery for the technological age'.[22] That it was conducted by criminals in multiple countries was a warning sign that this was not just a local problem, but spanned continents. It also pointed to some unpalatable truths about digital transformation.

Infrastructure

We can characterize most of the cyber threats that have emerged in recent decades as ways of targeting computers and data. In technical terms, this makes sense: there is no cyber version of crime or espionage without digital computers and data. But we have to ask about the ultimate purposes of these activities. Targeting digital systems is undertaken not because of the innate value of those systems but due to their economic, social and political worth to people, companies and societies. The globalization of information networks and their rapid embedding as transformational technologies means that they are now considered essential infrastructures for almost every aspect of contemporary life, particularly in the more technologically replete countries of the Global North. In dictionary terms, an infrastructure consists in the physical and organizational resources essential for enabling a greater activity or undertaking. We usually pay little attention to infrastructures like sewerage or electricity, until something goes wrong with these and other systems that support vital societal functions.

Cyber threats are one way of causing problems for the functionality or availability of infrastructures, which increasingly rely on digital systems. The Citibank heist of 1994 and the WannaCry scare of 2017 are a quarter of a century apart but each compromised the expected functioning of key systems, specifically financial and healthcare infrastructures. In the late 1990s public policy began to recognize, first, that infrastructures were worryingly vulnerable to a range of state and criminal cyber threats and, second, that our dependence on these systems was itself a source of vulnerability. Moreover, as the US asserted repeatedly, it was precisely those countries like itself that relied extensively on computer networks and systems for the delivery of key services that were most vulnerable to cyber threats.

Cyber was not the only concern during this period – the 11 September 2001 terrorist attacks played a key role in the US too – but governments began to think in terms of critical infrastructures, those systems upon which we had come to depend, and which were apparently so vulnerable to compromise and subversion. As many of these were reliant on digital technologies, cybersecurity became a key consideration in how these critical infrastructures could be protected and secured from internal and external cyber threats. Commonly, 'digital' is regarded as a critical infrastructure sector in its own right, but it is also the foundation upon which all other critical infrastructures rely. When the European Union identified 'critical information infrastructures' (CII) in 2005 as a first step towards mandating their security, it did so as follows: 'ICT [information and communications technology] that are Critical Infrastructures for themselves or that are essential for the operation of Critical Infrastructures (telecommunications, computers/software, Internet, satellites, and so on)'.[23] This captures the interdependence of cyber and other infrastructures, as well as the broad range of technologies that comprise critical information infrastructures, few of which are constrained by the conventional territorial boundaries of the state.

Countries differ in how they identify critical infrastructures, although a standard list would include: government, defence, civil nuclear, energy, water, food, communications, finance, health, transport, space, emergency services and so on. All are dependent upon cyber systems for delivering goods and services, whether at the operational level (the physical control of drinking water supplies: pipes, dams and reservoirs) or within the organizations that own and operate these systems (the business processes of the water company and its customers and contracts). A distinction is often made between operational technology (OT) and information technology (IT). OT interacts with the physical environment through devices like industrial control systems and safety mechanisms; IT manages the flow of information across and between business systems.[24] Each involves hardware and software, but their primary functions differ. Both, however, are vulnerable to cyber operations.

In 2021 the business IT systems of US company Colonial Pipeline were subject to a criminal ransomware operation, which led the company to shut down its OT systems, disrupting fuel supplies to the eastern seaboard of the United States for several days. The criminal group responsible was partially successful in extracting a ransom from Colonial Pipeline but cared little about the disruption caused to innocent citizens and businesses.[25] Consider an alternative scenario in which energy infrastructures were compromised by nation-state hackers rather than criminals. Here, disruption might be calibrated to cause fear or panic among a civilian population, thereby pressuring a government to change its behaviour in some fashion, such as acceding to a foreign state's demands. The intended effects are political, not financial, but the targets (OT/IT) and means (malware) are the same. For operations uncovered in their reconnaissance phase, it is nearly impossible to tell which is which: a single instance of malware is unlikely to tell the analyst if it is there for criminal or espionage purposes, or if it is a precursor to a more destructive operation.[26]

Not all cyber operations target infrastructures as such; most cybercriminality is much more modest in scope, and looks to exploit human foibles through low-level fraud and deception, rather than cause major disruption. However, the Internet as a network of networks can lay claim to being a global infrastructure of unparalleled reach and significance. Problems with this infrastructure – highlighted by the twin problems of dependence and vulnerability – are therefore global too. Critical infrastructures are usually designated as such at the national level, but their physical and virtual components are often interlinked across national borders. This is particularly the case for business systems, as multinational and transnational companies are involved in international logistics and supply chains or enable global finance flows through banking payment and clearance mechanisms, all of which have been regularly targeted.[27] Some analysts also worry about cyber-induced failure in one infrastructure locality or sector cascading into others, potentially causing a systemic crash in global information networks. We have yet to experience a total Internet outage – the architecture of the Internet somewhat mitigates against it – but there have been enough accidental outages of individual networks and platforms that one remains a possibility.[28] What would be the effects of such an outage on the everyday security of people all over the world? Who would be blamed and who would respond? What might be the impacts on national and international security?

Conclusion

This chapter has provided a brief tour of the development of computer systems and networks since the Second World War. Its main aim was to outline how the relationship between computers and security has become more complex over time. As for so many other technologies, national security was the driver and proving ground for early digital computers, which swiftly found novel applications in civilian life once the war ended. Security concerns extended beyond the demands of the state into the privacy of individuals and to what became classical 'information security', with its focus on confidentiality, integrity and availability. The globalization of information technologies ushered in large-scale digital transformation, our enthusiasm for which should be tempered by the realization that our digital dependency is also a source of acute vulnerability. Through the lens of infrastructure, we can see that digital systems and networks are critical infrastructures that underpin much of daily life and societal security. We are now at a point where cybersecurity is almost being asked to secure everything from the smallest device and dataset to the largest firms and most powerful countries – not on its own, of course, but its central infrastructural role is hard to deny and costly to ignore.

The following chapters look in more detail at four sets of issues that emerge from this framing of what cybersecurity is for. Chapter 4 will look at the politics and economics of national cybersecurity, in particular how governments and markets work together to address cybersecurity problems. Chapter 5 explores how cybersecurity is organized and contested on the international level. Chapter 6 addresses the ethical and human dimensions of cybersecurity. First, though, Chapter 3 provides an overview of the cyber threat landscape and sets out how cybersecurity aims to tackle it.

3
CYBERSECURITY, CYBER RISK

The preceding chapter outlined key aspects of the historical relationship between computers and security. The essential picture is that the networking of computers, allied to the demonstrable insecurity of computer networks, has helped create a situation in which our dependence on them is itself a significant vulnerability. The task of cybersecurity is to help manage that vulnerability in such a way as to capitalize on the benefits of digital transformation, rather than to buckle under its more problematic aspects, some of which were alluded to in the previous chapter. The problem, however, is that no one seriously believes that we can engineer digital networks in a way that will make cyber insecurity vanish. There are just too many bugs and errors of use and implementation in global cyberspace for this to be the case. Moreover, it is impossible to provide technical solutions that will thwart all the people and organizations looking to exploit these environments for their own ends, whether cybercriminals, hackers or hostile states. Technical cybersecurity can certainly help improve the overall levels of security in computer networks and systems, sometimes to a very high degree, but it can never deliver perfect cybersecurity. Old problems persist and new ones arise, particularly as the overall threat landscape is dynamic and ever-changing, reflecting the constant reconfiguration of digital environments.

This chapter sets out the cyber threat landscape in more detail and outlines some of the key approaches to countering it. There are two principal reasons why digital targets are selected: criminal and political. The first section outlines what we mean by criminal cyber threats and describes key actors and methods. Although this will not be a technical description, it will introduce some important cybersecurity terms that you will encounter throughout the book, such as malware and social engineering. The second section looks at political cyber threats, such as those from espionage and warfare, in which attackers' intentions are aligned with higher-level political ambitions, principally the pursuit of national interests in peace and war. The third section shows that cybersecurity intends to secure a range of different objects and has fundamental links with other forms of security. I offer a definition of cybersecurity that tries to cover these different aims and ambitions and to which we will return towards the end of the book. The fourth section builds on this understanding of cybersecurity to introduce the ideas of cyber risk and cyber resilience as ways of coping with the problems of cyber insecurity.

Criminal threats

Cybersecurity has long organized its thinking in relation to specific cyber threats, usually understood as distinct types of actor – individuals, groups or organizations – looking to achieve their goals through compromising digital networks and systems. As mentioned in the Introduction, this is not always very helpful. If your job is to defend, say, a corporate network from outside (or, sometimes, inside) threats, it matters less whether the attacker is a cybercriminal or foreign intelligence service than if you can work out what they did and how to fix it quickly. Identifying the attacker is secondary. However, if you are responsible for a military communications system, if may be essential to attribute rapidly, so you can provide decision-makers with timely intelligence about who to respond to, if necessary. Nevertheless, describing the main actors is one way of identifying what needs to be secured: different actors have different aims and will look to compromise different types of assets. At the same time, they often use similar methods to gain access and exploit information systems, sometimes referred to as tactics, techniques and procedures (TTPs), which means that criminal and political cyber operations can be difficult to distinguish without significant further investigation.

Cybercriminals view cyberspace and those who use it as potential sources of illicit revenue, as targets for fraud, theft and extortion.[1] A distinction is often made between cyber-dependent and cyber-enabled crimes (see Table 1). Cyber-dependent crimes include operations against data and systems that target computer systems, networks and data, and could not exist without those hardware components. Ransomware is an obvious example, as are various other forms of illegal access and data acquisition. Cyber-enabled crimes include 'old' forms of crime – fraud and theft, notably – committed through 'new' digital means. In practice, this is not always a useful point of difference, as actual cybercriminal operations combine the two, as we will see below.

Sometimes the target of cybercriminals might be a company, against which they can deploy ransomware – which encrypts corporate data until a ransom is paid and the data decrypted – and extract financial reward. Or they might steal sensitive commercial data and threaten to release it on the Internet unless payment is received. In each of these cases, victims have been known to pay up and still not get their data back. Other sources of revenue include stealing

Table 1: Types of cybercrime

Cyber-dependent crimes: 'crimes against the machine'	Cyber-enabled crimes: 'crimes using the machine'
Illegal access (hacking, cracking)	Computer-related fraud
Illegal acquisition of data in storage	Intellectual property theft
Illegal interception of data in transit	Phishing
Data or system interference	Identity theft
Ransomware, DDoS attacks, malware	Digital piracy
Cross-cutting: organized crime, dark markets, cybercrime-as-a-service	

customer data, like credit card details and personal information, and selling it on specialized web forums to other criminals, who then use it for various forms of fraud. There is a robust underground economy on the so-called dark web for these types of operations. Some criminals provide bespoke services to other criminals, leasing infrastructure or hacking tools and platforms to them, such as ransomware-as-a-service and malware-as-a-service, both lucrative sources of revenue.[2] Criminals, unsurprisingly, do not baulk at targeting public services or critical infrastructures like energy and communications, as long as they can reap financial reward. The startling ubiquity of ransomware operations against civilian networks is evidence of a concerning rise in attacks on the fabric of urban life and the services upon which millions rely. In 2021, over half of educational establishments surveyed across 31 countries were affected by ransomware operations, impacting teaching and learning, and leading to loss of intellectual property.[3] In August 2022, criminals demanded $10 million from a Paris hospital, a ransomware operation that crippled healthcare provision and forced authorities to move patients to other establishments.[4] Similar examples are increasing in frequency, with one study suggesting that ransomware operations against US healthcare facilities are leading to increased patient mortality.[5]

Cybercriminals also target individuals within companies, hoping that they divulge information like passwords that enable them to access corporate networks, or deceive everyday Internet users through diverse means of fraud and theft. Sometimes, this involves directing legitimate Internet traffic to fraudulent websites, where login credentials and credit card information are collected, by implanting malware on their machines, or by social engineering. Social engineering exploits human trust by psychologically manipulating users.[6] A common means is 'phishing' emails, which might appear to be from a genuine source – often a bank or tax office asking for verification of a previous transaction or personal details – but which dupe users into giving sensitive information, which can then be used to gain access to business systems or otherwise monetized. These are often high-volume spam email campaigns, which only require a few people to respond to attract a return on criminal investment. 'Spear-phishing' is more sophisticated, in that criminals target specific people, sometimes in senior leadership roles – when it is known as 'whaling' – pretending to be a colleague or client asking for information, which the unwitting individual sometimes provides. Related forms of fraud are also committed via SMS (text), voice calls and social media messaging, the incidence of which is increasing as more people access the Internet via smartphones and mobile devices.

There is a distinction in TTPs between the use of malicious software (malware) to enter a system and social engineering. Each exploits a vulnerability – if we can characterize human trust as such – through deceptive means. Deception is at the heart of most cybersecurity threats: either a computer is deceived into acting in a particular way, or a human is. This is why one commentator has written, 'There is, in the end, no forced entry in cyberspace. Whoever gets in enters through pathways produced by the system itself.'[7] If we think of people and machines as together comprising a sociotechnical system, this explains why both logical (computers) and cognitive (human) pathways are targeted for exploitation. In practice, many operations combine the two. Sometimes, users are tricked into doing the right thing, such as installing software updates, only to find subsequently that the updates themselves have been compromised in so-called supply chain attacks.[8]

Political threats

The preceding section does not exhaust the diversity and ingenuity of cybercriminals, who are widely regarded as the most prevalent and ubiquitous cyber threat. As the previous chapter indicated, though, computer networks can be exploited by actors with political aims, such as state militaries, intelligence agencies and hacktivists. Some would include potential cyberterrorists in this category, although thus far terrorists have found it easier and more impactful to create spectacular effects through more conventional means.[9] The same principles of deception apply for these political actors, although states in particular may have a wider array of useful resources on which to draw. If they want to enter a target system for the purposes of intelligence gathering or to disrupt operations, they must rely on deceiving logical or cognitive structures. As with criminals, they often do both.

When Dragonfly, a Russian group thought to be affiliated with Russian intelligence, seeks to compromise Western energy companies and regulators, as they have done since at least 2011, they use a combination of malware and social engineering to achieve their objectives.[10] A Chinese group reportedly uses ransomware to distract targets while they go elsewhere in the system to steal intellectual property.[11] During military operations against Islamic State (ISIS), US military and intelligence used phishing emails to gain access to ISIS systems, then deployed malware on those networks to map their internal structure. ISIS operators were then locked out of their accounts and forced to use less secure platforms, potentially making their physical locations visible and therefore more easily targeted by conventional military attacks.[12] In this case, cyber operations were designed to degrade ISIS's online operations and to flush its fighters out into the open, as well as to cause them psychological stress. The effects of these offensive cyber operations are therefore not restricted to the expected logical effects of disrupting computing assets but extend into manipulating adversaries' behaviours and decision-making. In the worst-case speculative scenarios of large-scale cyberwarfare against civilian populations – most likely through targeting critical infrastructures like food, water, transport and energy – the concern is that serious disruption would cause civil unrest and coerce governments to change their policy and strategy in line with an attacker's demands.

Economic advantage may well be a driving factor in some cyber operations but even these are motivated by political concerns: economic prosperity and political security are bound together very tightly. Keeping its burgeoning middle classes satisfied is important to the domestic legitimacy of the Chinese Communist Party, as is its great power status and achieving technological parity with the United States. Both find expression in its cyber operations. China has been responsible for extended campaigns of commercial cyberespionage, in which units of the People's Liberation Army (PLA) and others target specific economic sectors, often in North America and Europe, for the specific purpose of extracting intellectual property that China can then use to bolster its own strategic industries, including defence. The first widely known case of this was exposed in 2013 by US firm Mandiant and showed how PLA Unit 61398 in Shanghai was responsible for operations against 141 companies in twenty major industries outside China, mostly in the United States.[13] The term Advanced Persistent Threat (APT) is commonly used to describe groups like Unit 61398 (APT1), sophisticated state and state-backed groups which conduct long-term cyber operations against foreign targets, usually for purposes of intelligence-gathering and data exfiltration. Although notoriously difficult to corroborate – and always hotly denied by countries accused of harbouring them – several dozen APTs have been identified in China, Iran, Russia, Turkey, Israel, North Korea and elsewhere and, of course, what some observers wryly call APT0, the United States.[14] APTs often develop distinct TTPs, which skilled cyber threat intelligence analysts can see in their data over time and help others to recognize and counter.[15]

There is not always a clear-cut demarcation between criminal and political threats. States have at times undertaken cybercriminal acts and criminals are often employed by states to carry out actions that governments wish to keep deniable. In the first register, North Korea has sought to augment its meagre foreign currency earnings with operations against external bodies, particularly banks. In 2016 North Korea's state-allied Lazarus Group (APT38) attempted to transfer $1 billion from a US account belonging to the central bank of Bangladesh by subverting the international digital payment system SWIFT.[16] Thanks to some eagle-eyed bank employees, the overall mission was foiled but not before $81 million had been siphoned off to an account in the Philippines and then laundered through Macau; most of it has not been recovered. The WannaCry incident described in the Introduction was also a (failed) attempt by North Korea to extract money from criminal activities. For a country beset by sanctions and short of foreign currency, cybercrime was a rational – if illegal – option for its leadership. In a slightly different vein, it is alleged that Russia allows cybercrime groups to operate from its territory and in neighbouring post-Soviet states, as long as they target only foreign entities and provide kickbacks to the relevant officials and gatekeepers, including the Russian military.[17] Along with other countries, Russia is not averse to hiring and directing a range of proxy actors, including cybercriminals, to conduct cyber operations against its adversaries.[18]

Countries on the receiving end of such operations have not been shy in linking economic and criminal cyber threats to national security. In the first half of 2021, capitalizing on a pronounced shift to remote working during COVID-19, it is estimated that £754 million was stolen online from UK bank customers. In addition to the significant personal and commercial harm caused, some believe this should now be treated as a national security threat.[19] When Russian cybercriminals conducted a ransomware operation against Colonial Pipeline in 2021, causing significant disruption to US east coast fuel supplies, some senators called it an act of war and demanded that the perpetrators be hunted down and executed.[20] Although this was a minority view, it served a deliberate political function: blaming the administration of President Joe Biden for not taking the cybersecurity of US critical infrastructure seriously enough. It should also be apparent that there are risks in such escalatory rhetoric: espionage and war are not equivalent and should not be conflated in this way.[21] However, it indicates that cyber threats blur the boundaries between law enforcement, economic security, national security and geopolitics.

So what is cybersecurity?

Given the diversity of cyber threats outlined above, what is the role of cybersecurity in countering them? What do we mean by cybersecurity at all? We will explore the answers to these questions in more detail in subsequent chapters, but we should establish first the broad parameters of cybersecurity. This requires exploring how cybersecurity is defined and by whom. This is not an easy task, principally because the cast of cybersecurity actors is very diverse, each of whom has professional responsibilities or inclinations that prioritize some aspects of cybersecurity over others. This means that experts in one field can quite easily talk past experts in another. The range of cybersecurity problems is also extensive and most definitions quickly become long and unwieldy. As an initial step towards resolving this, it is useful to distinguish between two related but distinct meanings of cybersecurity.

The first is that cybersecurity relates to the relative security of cyberspace itself. Not everyone likes the term cyberspace, but it refers to the physical and virtual components of informational environments like the Internet. Cybersecurity is therefore the security of hardware, software and data and the diverse digital environments enabled by their complex interactions and dependencies. The second register concerns how the security of cyberspace is attained and includes all the technical and nontechnical means of doing so. On one hand, therefore, cybersecurity is a desirable condition; on the other, it is the process of achieving that condition. This seems relatively straightforward, but there is substantial disagreement about what each of these means in practice, particularly when we consider that cybersecurity is deeply linked to much more than computers and computer networks.

One way to approach this is in terms of how influential communities frame cybersecurity. There is much variation within and between these groups, but each characteristically prioritizes the security of a particular object, to which cybersecurity can contribute. At the heart of cybersecurity is a long-standing concern with information security (infosec): the protection of information and information systems from unauthorized or inappropriate access. Infosec professionals have many and varied roles, but all work towards implementing and maintaining technical measures to protect information and information technologies. The core 'referent objects' (see Table 2) of their security practices are computers, computer networks and data, which they secure against a range of threats. Some of these are intentional, such as cybercrime or so-called insider threats (employees or contractors looking to leak sensitive information to the outside world). It also includes mitigating the inadvertent mistakes of users, like opening an email laced with malware or visiting a malicious website. They must also deal with errors of code and programming, which occur in all software and hardware configurations. They are very often the first responders to security problems arising in complex IT systems and networks and are essential to how individuals and organizations thrive and survive in the digital ecosystem. A huge industry has grown up around information security, providing goods (anti-virus software, firewalls) and services (consultancy, training) to organizations across the public and private sectors.

Even here, though, computer systems are not being secured for their own sake. They exist to support

Table 2: Referent objects of cybersecurity, showing their relations with the main cyber threats and cybersecurity actors

	Main emphasis			
	Information security	Economic security	Political security	National security
Referent objects	Computer systems, computer networks, data Privacy	Economic prosperity	Political order Critical infrastructures	Nation/state Critical infrastructures Military capability
Main threats	Cybercriminal Hackers Hacktivists	Cybercriminal Cyberespionage (commercial)	Cybercriminal Cyberespionage (strategic) Cyberwarfare	Cyberwarfare Cyberespionage (strategic)
Main actors	Cybersecurity industry	Business/private sector Intelligence Law enforcement	Government Intelligence Law enforcement	Government Intelligence Military
Keywords	Confidentiality, integrity, availability Business continuity	Economic stability Economic growth	Government Homeland security	Geopolitics Diplomacy War

business operations, for example, so infosec serves the higher-level objective of sustaining commercial value. This is why cybersecurity should be on the agenda of all managers and executives. Without cybersecurity awareness and investment, companies expose themselves to disruption to their businesses and reputations. It is also a matter of public policy, therefore, as governments exhort their business communities to improve cybersecurity against cybercrime and commercial cyberespionage threats. This is cybersecurity as economic security, the referent object of which is national economic prosperity through stability and growth. Law enforcement plays a crucial role here, within the limits of its overstretched budgets, as it targets organized cybercrime groups and other threats to the national economic fabric. Intelligence agencies are also involved, especially when economic cyber threats emerge from nation-state contexts, as with China, North Korea and others.

Cybersecurity is also about securing domestic political order and national well-being. If foreign actors target critical infrastructures like health, energy, transport and communications through cyber means, they could seriously disrupt everyday life for millions of people, as well as the ability of governments to deliver social security and preserve law and order. In the US, critical infrastructure protection falls under the purview of 'homeland security', a designation that is increasingly used in other jurisdictions too. The types of APTs and cybercriminals that regularly target critical infrastructures – including democratic functions like electoral systems – are squarely on the radar of intelligence agencies and law enforcement, most of whom are active members of transnational arrangements that share threat intelligence and operational capacity. Cybersecurity shifts here from the operational level to something properly strategic, as it helps secure society from cyber threats and the range of possible effects resonating far beyond cyberspace itself.

We see this even more clearly in the activities of military and intelligence agencies and national diplomatic corps. For these groups, cybersecurity is a means to secure the nation-state from foreign digital espionage and hostile attacks on critical infrastructures, national military capabilities and other strategic assets. This is cybersecurity as national security. Diplomats work to smooth over the disagreements that emerge between nations on these issues, as well as promote visions of international order that – hopefully – encourage international security and geopolitical stability. (We will examine these dynamics in Chapter 5.)

Cybersecurity, then, means slightly different things to different communities. All agree that cybersecurity fundamentally involves the security of computer networks, systems and data (broadly, cyberspace), but their primary objectives vary across social, economic and political contexts. This makes it difficult to find a common definition of cybersecurity that works for everyone. As a placeholder, I want to suggest this provisional definition: cybersecurity is the security one enjoys in, from and through cyberspace, and the measures taken to achieve this. This is far from perfect – let alone snappy – but captures the fact that cybersecurity is a condition *and* a process, and that it helps to secure more than just cyberspace. It also hints that cybersecurity is not just about protection or defence but might be a means of proactively getting what you want in other areas of life too, as subsequent chapters will demonstrate.

Cyber risk and resilience

When we think about any form of security, it is with reference to protecting something from a threat. Cybersecurity protects an entity – a computer network, a firm, the economy, the nation – from cyber threats of diverse kinds. Yet, we have seen that perfect cybersecurity is not possible: sometimes a threat will succeed. There are always vulnerabilities that can be exploited. If this realization is not to turn into fatalism – why bother with cybersecurity if it will eventually fail? – how do cybersecurity professionals make sense of this? One overarching framework for approaching cybersecurity has emerged in recent years: cyber risk. Risk and security are not quite the same. If security is about doing things right, risk is about doing the right things. Cybersecurity is essentially about computer systems, but how do we know what to prioritize, where to invest our money and effort, and to what end? Cyber risk helps with all these dimensions of decision-making, from the individual to the company and the nation.

The classical approach to risk presents it as an equation:

$$risk = threat \times vulnerability \times impact$$

If we are a company looking to manage cyber risk – for example, a supplier of electricity to the civilian energy grid – we look ahead at the cyber threats we are likely to face. We know from experience that cybercriminals and APTs target our sector, so we scan the horizon and begin to develop a profile of known and expected cyber threats to electricity companies like ours. At the same time, we must look inwards at the company itself, its networks and systems, and at our employees, clients and supply chains, and work out where our vulnerabilities lie. Can we be sure that everyone – from the ledger clerk to the executive board – is doing their bit for our cybersecurity? Do they understand issues of physical and IT security? Are their passwords on a sticky note on their monitor? Do employees work remotely and are they trained to do so safely and securely? Does the board regularly discuss cybersecurity, or do they delegate it to the techies? We must then ask: what will be the impact if we get hit by a significant cyber incident? How will it affect our business continuity? Will it cause downtime and financial loss and how can these be quantified and mitigated? Can be sure that we will not be subject to legal or regulatory enquiry if it turns out we were negligent or complacent?

These are the questions posed by any competent risk analysis, along with many others, and they are sometimes uncomfortable for an organization to address. Taken together, they indicate what decisions an organization's leaders need to take about what they hold of value, what they must prioritize and what investment they require in technical cybersecurity, staff training, insurance products and much more. Getting to grips with exposure to cyber risk is a key responsibility of leadership. As many executives have found, ignoring or underplaying cyber risk is poor practice. When the databases of consumer credit reporting agency Equifax were breached in 2017, exposing the personal details of nearly 150 million Americans, its CEO attempted to blame anyone but himself, while bungling the company's response. His retirement followed swiftly. Had he taken personal responsibility for cyber risk as a core aspect of Equifax business – a company that makes its profits from secure data processing – a robust cyber risk management strategy could have averted some of the worst aspects of the incident.[22] Businesses cannot eradicate threats like cybercriminals and APTs, but they can manage down vulnerabilities and reduce the impact to their organizations. In so doing, they reduce their exposure to cyber risk.

A related approach is cyber resilience. Again, this assumes that negative cyber incidents will occur, despite the best efforts of cybersecurity and cyber risk management processes. The key, therefore, is to ensure that organizations can continue to deliver their key services as best as they can under conditions of often severe stress. This is particularly important for critical infrastructure operators like banks and energy suppliers, as well as water, food and transport services. This is neatly encapsulated by the British domestic intelligence agency MI5's possibly apocryphal assertion that society is only 'four meals away from anarchy'. Whether this is a real planning assumption of the UK government is debatable, but it illustrates the fine line between business as usual and the ability of society to handle sudden adversity. Cyber resilience is promoted as an ongoing process of preparing for cyber incidents, absorbing their impact when they happen, recovering as quickly as possible and learning from the experience to adapt processes for potential future problems. The shift to remote digital working during the COVID-19 pandemic heightened sensitivity to cyber resilience. In the European Union, for instance, the European Commission president Ursula von der Leyen noted in 2021 that 'If everything is connected, everything can be hacked', supercharging the EU cyber resilience agenda, supported by new transnational legislation.[23]

This links to a broader observation about cyber risk. Large technological systems like the Internet are so complex that dynamics emerge that are unpredicted and unpredictable. There are so many interconnected nodes and so much data, all plagued with errors of design or implementation, that we should also think in terms of systemic cyber risk.[24] Interdependence brings with it the possibility that an incident in one place might cause failures elsewhere, potentially cascading out across multiple sectors. An event in cyberspace might cause physical and

Figure 3: The cyber resilience process

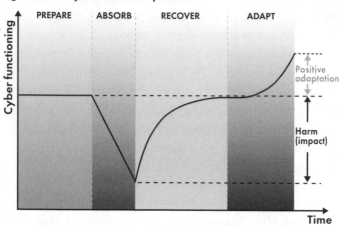

psychological effects in the real world. Conversely, physically disrupting a server or cloud storage facility would cause problems for data exchange and the services that depend on it. The infamous Northeast electrical blackout of 2003 was caused by a combination of physical disruption, software problems and human error, rippling across several US states and into Canada. It took days to restore power in some areas.[25] In October 2021 misconfiguration of a Facebook system accidentally took the platform offline for several hours, as well as WhatsApp and Instagram.[26] This attracted some schadenfreude from those frustrated by Facebook's market dominance and sceptical of its motives, but consider the many millions of people who use these platforms for work, leisure and essential communications. We can begin to discern the longer-term systemic implications of a few misplaced ones and zeroes, let alone the impact of deliberate attacks on critical infrastructures and important digital platforms.

Conclusion

This chapter has set out the broad landscape of criminal and political cyber threats and some of the ways to manage it. Cybersecurity is essentially about protecting computer systems, networks and data, but the specific rationales of various actors differ according to their roles and responsibilities. This is why it is so difficult to define cybersecurity, although I have offered a provisional definition of it above. The chapter has also outlined the parameters of cyber risk management as a way of identifying and prioritizing cybersecurity needs. Although this mainly focused on corporate entities, the same approach can be used for individuals and nations too. The digital 'attack surface' is growing fast, particularly as more and more devices become interconnected through the Internet of Things (IoT), the massive deployment of computing devices in everyday objects that send and receive data across the Internet.[27] We must also consider the well-known capacities of criminals and state agencies to adapt to and exploit novel technologies, from artificial intelligence, blockchain and advances in computing, each of which has implications for cybersecurity. Addressing cybersecurity and cyber risk will only become more important in future, hence the need for conceptual and practical tools to manage them.

In the next chapter, we look at how these frameworks are put into practice. As is apparent from this book so far, there are many players in cybersecurity, who sometimes disagree about their roles and responsibilities. One of the most important relationships in cybersecurity is between the state and the market. This brings into focus the distinct and sometimes misaligned interests of the public and private sectors and their effects on cybersecurity. Chapter 4 looks at the politics and economics of national cybersecurity, how governments and firms work together in public–private partnerships to improve cybersecurity and how their respective activities sometimes undermine it.

4
STATES AND MARKETS

S o far, this book has made the case that cybersecurity is as much political as it is technical. This is not just because 'all security is political' but because cybersecurity is entangled with economic, national and international security, each of which has inherently political dimensions. As the history outlined in Chapter 2 demonstrates, computers have been wrapped up in the worlds of security since their invention. They have also, in a concrete sense, enabled new forms of behaviour with security implications, such as cybercrime, cyberespionage and cyberwarfare. Chapter 3 described this cyber threat landscape and some aspects of the proposed response, specifically cybersecurity and cyber risk management. This is useful background, but who decides what is required and who puts it into practice? Sometimes, the responsibility for steering cybersecurity rests with governments, legislatures and international organizations, with other parties left to implement policy or adjust their practices to meet legal and regulatory requirements. At other times, it is nongovernmental organizations or industry that lead the way in developing cybersecurity solutions. Little of this happens without tensions emerging between important actors, either as a result of practical considerations or because they differ in how they think cybersecurity should be addressed.

One key distinction is between public- and private-sector actors. The public sector describes those organizations owned, controlled and funded by government to provide public services, such as armed forces, central banks, police and national health authorities. The private sector consists of commercial entities – companies, firms – that are owned by private individuals and generally operate on a for-profit basis. This is a common way of discerning different corporate objectives – public service versus private profit – although it is sometimes difficult to tell where the public sector ends and the private sector begins. This is particularly true in political contexts where there is little meaningful distinction between the two, as in centrally planned economies or where private companies provide public services. Nevertheless, it is a useful departure point for this chapter, in which we look at the politics and economics of cybersecurity through the lens of public–private interaction.

In the first section, we take a step back and look at who makes the rules for cybersecurity. Public policy is developed by governments, but other actors help set the agenda, including non-governmental organizations and companies. The second section looks in greater depth at the relationship between the public and private sectors, particularly the perpetually vexed issue of how to align commercial and public service motivations. Section three provides insight into a particular set of cybersecurity working arrangements known as public–private partnerships (PPPs). These come in many forms and are useful ways of pooling expertise and resources to solve public policy problems, although they sometimes struggle, particularly when public and private actors need to share sensitive information. The final section offers some thoughts about the darker side of public–private interaction, including what some have termed a 'cyber-industrial complex' and the development of an international market in digital surveillance technologies. Taken together, these issues provide a brief overview of the cybersecurity interdependencies of states and markets.

Who makes the rules?

Governments make policy to solve economic, social and political problems. Public policy usually takes the form of a statement of priorities and objectives, accompanied by an outline of what activities are required to meet those objectives in a given timeframe. These measures commonly include new organizations or the streamlining of old ones, new funding streams paid for through taxation, and regulation. Governments can determine the direction and resourcing of these tasks but in democratic countries need legislatures to pass any laws necessary to achieving their ambitions.

Stakeholders – everyone with an interest in a particular policy field – then work out how to align themselves with public policy and maximize their gains within the new framework.

This is what we could term a top-down approach to public policy and we see it often in cybersecurity. Two decades ago, few countries had recognizable cybersecurity policies; now, at least 120 countries have issued high-level policy statements that attempt to align resources with cybersecurity objectives.[1] This tells us little about the efficacy of these policies, but it is indicative of the seriousness with which countries view cybersecurity, as well as their desire to be seen to be doing something about it. Some lower-income countries, for instance, can offer little in the way of public investment but are keen to show their commitment to what is increasingly viewed as a marker of national maturity.[2]

These policies differ greatly in their scope, ambition and specificity. Some are little more than wish-lists; most are short on details of how to achieve their objectives; all are criticized by fellow professionals and commentators for one reason or another, as is normal for public policy. They are also authored by different government departments, depending on a country's institutional structure and cybersecurity challenges. These priorities will shift over time, particularly as the importance of cybersecurity rises on domestic political agendas. Brazil has historically given its military primary responsibility for cybersecurity, although its principal problem has been cybercrime, which the police and judiciary might be better placed to address. It has recently, therefore, bolstered the ability of central government to coordinate public-sector cybersecurity functions.[3] It is not uncommon for an initial high-level strategy to spawn subsequent separate but interlinked policies for distinct themes or sectors. The UK's Cabinet Office has been the central coordinator of British cybersecurity since the late 2000s but delegates responsibilities to multiple government departments, such as defence, business, home affairs and foreign policy, which produce subsidiary policy documents of their own.[4]

Despite the diversity of national policies, they share a central aim: to develop unity of effort in pursuit of national cybersecurity goals. Policies set the rules of the game for everyone involved, which sometimes become formalized as law and regulation. This is always difficult, as there are many stakeholders to consider across the public and private sectors. This leads to tensions between government departments, and between government and external partners. There is a further complication, in that governments are not the only ones to make rules in cyberspace. They can define national objectives for cyber defence, cyber resilience, cyber diplomacy and foreign policy, investment in skills and so on, but cyberspace operates according to other rules too.

As we saw in Chapter 2, the Internet was founded on technical protocols and architectures that were developed largely outside the purview of states. It remains technical experts who determine most of the rules for global data exchange, hardware and software specifications, and international standards. The majority of these expert communities are invisible to most Internet users. The Internet Engineering Task Force (IETF), which maintains the technical standards of TCP/IP, is not any better known to the public than the World Wide Web Consortium (W3C) and its stewardship of Web standards. These organizations grew out of community need rather than government policy, becoming transnational actors in ways that states struggled to be in this environment. The Internet Society (ISOC), for instance, was founded in 1992 when the US government relinquished control of some aspects of Internet administration. Much later, the US would – somewhat reluctantly – resign its nominal authority over the Internet Corporation for Assigned Names and Numbers (ICANN) and Internet Assigned Numbers Authority (IANA), which ensure that Internet traffic gets where it needs to efficiently. Not all of what these non-profits do is directly related to cybersecurity, but cybersecurity operates in an environment created and constrained by them. Governments can shape what happens in cyberspace much more easily than they can tinker with the architecture and rules of cyberspace itself. Periodic calls to re-engineer the Internet for better political security are usually therefore met with significant scepticism.[5]

The other important driver of cybersecurity is the market. It is not that the market sets the rules of cybersecurity per se, but that cybersecurity is dependent on the market for success. Government agencies are repositories of significant experience and expertise, on which they draw for operational acumen and policy development. What they are less good at is providing innovative cybersecurity solutions at pace and scale, so they turn to the private sector for help. Moreover, most of global cyberspace is owned or operated by private companies, so governments are restricted in the amount of direct authority they can exert, except through law and regulation. As mentioned previously, there are tensions between the public and private sectors, so what is the role of the market in cybersecurity?

The role of the private sector

There are circumstances in which governments are best placed to drive change in relatively straightforward fashion. Military affairs is one area in which governments can decide on strategic and budgetary priorities, allocate resources and direct state employees (service personnel, civil servants) in the required fashion. The state owns the military materiel (supplies, equipment, weapons) and determines who to buy them from and how to use them. This is very different from cybersecurity. It is clear from the history of cyberspace and cybersecurity that the private sector is the main driver of technological innovation – despite the government-funded origins of the Internet – and, for the last forty years, has been the main provider of digital infrastructure, hardware and software. Private companies are the principal operators of global telecommunications connectivity through terrestrial broadband networks, satellites and the nearly five hundred submarine cables through which most of the world's data traffic is routed between continents.[6] Although there is local variation, it is reckoned that approximately 90 per cent of the world's digital networks and systems is owned and operated by private companies, not governments. A similar figure applies to critical infrastructures that rely on digital connectivity to provide key societal functions. Governments recognize that this poses a challenge to their decision-making: companies are influential stakeholders in the cybersecurity ecosystem, but how can their interests be aligned with those of the state?

The central problem is that companies may lack incentives to invest in cybersecurity if they perceive that they have to shoulder the costs of security while sharing the benefits of that security with 'free-riding' partners. This situation is compounded by a lack of understanding of cyber risk in many companies, plus a determination to get products to market rapidly, perhaps by skimping on security measures. Since 2016 the infamous Mirai malware has leveraged insecure IoT devices like home surveillance cameras and broadband routers to conduct attacks on a range of targets. These devices are marketed as cheap consumer goods, often with default passwords such as '0000' or 'password', if they use passwords at all. Mirai scans the Internet for such devices, cracking their weak password protection, and harnesses them into what is called a botnet, a network of 'zombie' computers that are then used to direct massive volumes of network traffic at target systems. These distributed denial-of-service (DDoS) events overload their targets with communications requests, effectively rendering them unavailable (the 'A' of the CIA triad). In late 2016 Mirai DDoS attacks against US company Dyn – which acts a bit like a telephone directory for the Internet – caused outages to dozens of major Internet platforms, including Amazon, the BBC, PayPal and Spotify.[7] A month later, Mirai operators attempted to knock out mobile communications in Liberia.[8] People have been arrested and jailed for Mirai attacks but, because the malware source code is available online and poorly secured IoT devices continue to be sold, the malware and the attacks which it enables persist.

This and many other incidents have prompted change in government attitudes to business. Early iterations of the UK National Cyber Security Strategy, for example, were keen to promote industry as the provider of cybersecurity solutions rather than implement new law or regulation. In 2016 its new strategy admitted that 'looking to the market to drive secure cyber behaviours [...] has not achieved the scale and pace of change required to stay ahead of the fast moving threat.'[9] It led to a closer working relationship between government and industry and the translation into UK law in 2018 of the European Union's Network and Information Systems Directive, which puts greater pressure on digital service providers to raise their levels of cybersecurity or risk punitive measures. In 2021 it introduced specific IoT legislation that would, among other measures, ban universal default passwords in IoT devices.[10]

Law and regulation are not intended to be antagonistic to industry, although firms often push back against increased legislation and regulation, which they perceive as hindering their commercial freedom. Governments recognize that the private sector is the main source of security innovation and seek to encourage this through industrial policy that supports innovation and views the cybersecurity sector as a driver and enabler of economic growth in its own right.[11] Governments are also customers in this ecosystem, relying on the market to meet their cybersecurity needs, particularly for consultancy, incident response, and for bespoke services like 'penetration testing'. 'Pen testers' are authorized to hack into a computer system, thereby exposing vulnerabilities in configuration or process that can be remedied before a real incident occurs.[12] This is another aspect of the risk analysis and management posture expected of responsible organizations, public or private, which guides their cybersecurity priorities and investment decisions. There is, of course, an enormous market in business-to-business (B2B) cybersecurity, spanning a vast array of consultancy and advisory services, cyber insurance products, hardware and software solutions, network defence, training and much else, plus a substantial consumer anti-virus and firewall market.

The perpetual balancing act is between governments promoting cybersecurity as a national requirement and companies being incentivized to help with that project, which might not have an obvious profit angle and, some argue, might stifle innovation. Cybersecurity firms are happy to sell into this market – that is their business model – but other corporate entities can be harder to convince. US firms, for instance, have long been resistant to government cybersecurity intervention, as has the federal government itself.[13] Different dynamics exist in jurisdictions where the public–private distinction is less sustainable, like China: when the Chinese government sets cybersecurity policy, its 'private' sector follows.[14]

Public–private partnerships

Government and industry have differing approaches to cybersecurity, dependent on what they perceive as its primary purpose and their different strengths. Yet they have found productive ways to work with one another outside the conventional hierarchical relationships of law and regulation. Public–private partnerships (PPPs) are widely regarded as a key mode of cooperative working between government, private operators of critical infrastructure and the wider cybersecurity industry. PPPs emerged in the 1970s and 1980s as a way for governments to embrace 'market discipline' and neoliberal values in the delivery of public services, while also shifting risk from the taxpayer to private actors, which are rewarded if they fulfil their contractual obligations to deliver those services. In simpler terms, PPPs are cooperative ventures between the state and business, and can take many forms, as they do in cybersecurity. Some are relatively informal or voluntary; others are more contractual, like the pen testing and other services mentioned above; all involve trade-offs between public and private objectives.[15]

PPPs can involve the establishment of new institutions with specific responsibilities for cybersecurity and critical infrastructure protection. Estonia's Information System Authority was founded in 2011 to bring government and several dozen critical infrastructure operators under one roof with responsibility for protecting key services. It is paid for by public funds with industry contributing expertise and personnel on a voluntary basis.[16] This type of PPP is usually quite long-term, but others may be convened for shorter periods or to address areas of narrower focus. For example, committees consisting of government, industry and academics have been brought together to help develop national cybersecurity strategy in Austria, the Netherlands and Slovakia.[17] Other schemes may involve the secondment of industry personnel into government agencies to tackle emerging security problems, such as the UK's Industry 100 initiative.[18] All these PPPs serve an additional purpose in building trust between communities, an essential component of cybersecurity as a team sport. This does not, of course, mean there is universal agreement within a given PPP but that the main players consent to its pivotal role in resolving disagreements.

All cybersecurity PPPs involve the exchange of information, perhaps through the sharing of expertise or cyber threat intelligence that can help all parties to the arrangement. Governments can draw on their strategic intelligence capabilities to provide sometimes very detailed assessments of the activities and capabilities of hostile cyber actors. Industry – through its client relationships – can do the same from the perspective of victims of cyberespionage and cybercrime, as it has access to corporate networks not readily available to most governments for legal–constitutional reasons. Putting these sources together can benefit government and industry decision-making, contributing to better cybersecurity across public and private sectors, particularly if information is shared in real time.[19]

One well-known example is the UK's Cyber Security Information Sharing Partnership (CiSP), launched in 2013 to allow British firms and government agencies to share cyber threat intelligence in a secure and confidential environment. From relatively modest beginnings, it now involves over five thousand organizations across the UK, including firms operating in all formally denominated critical infrastructure sectors. CiSP is no cybersecurity panacea – like all PPPs, its effectiveness relies on long-term commitment, measurable objectives and the ability to demonstrate worth to both sides – but it has enhanced the sharing of cyber threat intelligence and enabled stakeholders to improve their cyber risk management processes.[20] There are similar Information Sharing and Analysis Centres (ISACs) and platforms around the world, serving countries, specific industrial sectors and the international community.[21] Computer emergency response teams (CERTs, which were briefly mentioned in Chapter 2) and related incident response organizations are PPPs in countries as diverse as

Hungary and Kenya, and are a common model for sector-specific teams.

Serious conflicts do arise that prevent information-sharing and illustrate the sometimes-stark differentiation between public and private goals and wider societal attitudes to government data access. US federal legislation to facilitate information-sharing between the US government and technology companies has often struggled to gain widespread support. The tech industry cites possible threats to users' privacy as sufficient reason to object, as well as a lack of clarity around precisely how federal agencies would use the data. Civil society groups – particularly in the wake of former National Security Agency contractor Edward Snowden's disclosures of US digital surveillance practices in the 2000s and beyond – have articulated similar suspicions, as have legislators opposed to potential state access to personal data. Set alongside historical surveillance malpractices and major data breaches, these were not unreasonable objections. The exfiltration by China of millions of federal US employees' security clearance data in 2014, for example, continues to cast a shadow over the efficacy of US cybersecurity in general.[22] US attitudes are also informed by a laissez-faire, hands-off approach to cybersecurity, in which regulation is considered the enemy of commerce. Successive US administrations have therefore sought to soothe privacy concerns and reassure industry that government intervention, while inevitable, will be as light as practically possible and respectful of the market's aversion to burdensome regulation.

There should be no assumption that public and private will always engage in cooperative cybersecurity ventures, even if most people believe they must. State and industry are internally very diverse and, while they already work together in myriad ways to achieve positive cybersecurity goals, including through PPPs, it is a persistent challenge to square away competing objectives and learn to live with operational and commercial trade-offs. Governments attempt to steer this process to meet the top-level objectives of cybersecurity, chief of which is national security, but the market is a powerful shaper of cybersecurity in general.

Market problems

There is another aspect to the interplay of private- and public-sector cybersecurity. For all the utility of PPPs and the like, there are less visible and more concerning dimensions to the relationship between state and market. While they should not dominate our overall understanding of cybersecurity, they present challenges to who or what we think cybersecurity is for. To do this requires that we pivot from thinking about cybersecurity as a protective notion to something aligned with the active pursuit of national objectives. In this sense, we return to the definition of cybersecurity from Chapter 3 as the security one enjoys in, from and through cyberspace, and the measures taken to achieve this. This implies that cyberspace might just be a platform used to pursue other forms of security, as we are indeed seeing in cybersecurity policy and practice. For example, the UK is one of the countries to acknowledge openly an offensive cyber capability, which is but one way of the UK using 'cyber as a way to protect and promote our interests in a landscape being reshaped by technology'.[23] Other countries are using similar military-intelligence cyber capabilities for espionage and disruption, even though they deny they are doing so. It is a matter of some debate whether these are legitimate tools, especially if they affect civilians and civilian infrastructures. The concern over the market in this context is its central role in what some term a growing 'cyber-industrial complex' that supports military cyberwarfare, digital espionage, domestic surveillance and other practices deemed potentially corrosive of human rights.[24]

This argument builds on US President Dwight Eisenhower's speech on leaving office in 1961. He warned against a growing 'military–industrial complex' that threatened to negatively influence public policy. The military would benefit from greater sophistication and volume of materiel; industry would profit from supplying it. Eisenhower's concern was that this dynamic would be self-perpetuating, led by profit and the desire for new military capabilities, rather than by objective military need. A similar argument is made for offensive cyber capabilities today, which in the eyes of some commentators are being led by the shiny new objects of cyberwarfare and espionage, not by strategic or operational necessity.[25] There is also, as Eisenhower suggested in the case of the military–industrial complex, a revolving door in cybersecurity, in which public officials rotate out of office into cybersecurity firms that then lobby governments for contracts. Sometimes these individuals end up back in public service. This is often a good way of keeping talent in the cybersecurity ecosystem, but it also fuels suspicions about undue corporate influence on public policy and the awarding of government contracts.

Some countries exploit the ambiguity around the meaning of cybersecurity, which provides cover for practices of digital surveillance and monitoring that would not normally be included under its umbrella.[26] This includes authoritarian states in the Gulf and the Middle East, Iran and China, but also democracies such as Israel, which has a robust domestic tech industry. Its infamous NSO Group markets 'spyware' to countries like Mexico, Pakistan, Rwanda and Kazakhstan.[27] Other companies, including in the US, Europe and India, sell products and services that also facilitate domestic surveillance of political opponents, journalists and civil society, usually masquerading as counterterrorism or crime-fighting capabilities.[28] This is cybersecurity as political security, prioritizing the survival of political regimes over human rights and human security. From the user's perspective, these capabilities are a way of pursuing national security through offensive cybersecurity and espionage. The victim's point of view might be quite different (see Chapter 6). In addition to legally constituted arrangements, there are also unregulated illicit markets in hacking goods and services that operate on the dark web, beyond the reach of search engines and the casual web user. They use encrypted peer-to-peer networks that require software specifically designed for anonymity and allow criminals to trade illegal goods and services, including knowledge of cyber vulnerabilities and the tools to exploit them. Governments are known to operate on these platforms, as investigators and customers. Government purchasing power helps sustain the economics of these markets, which lends an unresolved 'grey' tinge to what would otherwise look like distinctly black markets in hacking tools.[29]

Economically, private-sector cybersecurity is a success, but there is another major implication for the public sector. As the cybersecurity industry grows – market analytics suggest a global market of around $200 billion presently – it requires more skilled employees every year. Estimates of a global shortfall of 3.5 million personnel are common.[30] To attract workers, cybersecurity firms offer pay and conditions far better than the public sector can afford, compounding labour shortages in government agencies responsible for cybersecurity. Government recruitment therefore stresses the values of public service and the excitement of the cybersecurity 'mission', while public policy tackles skills, training, education and how to establish career pathways into cybersecurity, which is more and more being framed as a profession in its own right.[31] This is a major challenge for public-sector cybersecurity, as it implies that more public functions will, of necessity, be contracted out to the private sector. This is a reasonable and efficient approach to many aspects of defensive cybersecurity but presents ethical and legal problems for offensive cybersecurity.[32]

Conclusion

The politics and economics of cybersecurity are far more complex than this chapter can possibly address. Each country, government, industrial sector and company has different priorities and problems, all of which need to be taken into account in developing effective approaches to cybersecurity. If there are rules for pursuing and achieving cybersecurity, these are not the preserve of states alone. Governments attempt to drive public policy in the national interest, while acknowledging that expertise and innovation are more often found in the private sector and in non-profit organizations and academia. Finding ways to work together, including PPPs, is therefore a key policy priority, as are laws and regulations that do not stifle the strengths of the market. The central puzzle is how to align profit and the public interest, although the two are not necessarily mutually exclusive in either open or closed economies.

This chapter has also introduced some problematic aspects of the state–market relationship that impinge on cybersecurity, such as a nascent cyber-industrial complex and international markets in cyber technologies that undermine human rights in repressive regimes. The point is not that all of these intelligence and law enforcement activities are unjustified in all contexts – although some civil society actors make that precise case – but that we need to remain mindful of the relationships between states and markets under the guise of cybersecurity. I have included a brief discussion of these issues here because they pose a set of questions, not answers. It raises questions about the place of citizens – you and me – in cybersecurity, a theme that will be developed further in Chapter 6.

National perspectives will only take us so far in understanding the role of cybersecurity in the modern world. No country is so isolated that its decisions can ignore its global dimensions. After all, the digital infrastructures at its heart are transnational, as are many of the companies that make them work. The politics and economics of cybersecurity exist within an international order of states and international organizations, and within a global marketplace. States are constantly jockeying for position in these international structures: this is the purpose of foreign policy and diplomacy and is the context in which national interests are pursued, including in cybersecurity. The next chapter looks at the international dimensions of cybersecurity, a set of issues that shows how consequential political visions of cybersecurity have become.

5

INTERNATIONAL CYBERSECURITY

The previous chapter looked at states and markets and how the aims of cybersecurity are addressed in the context of critical infrastructures, and economic and national security. It described how the competing interests of important actors are managed through arrangements such as public–private partnerships. It revealed tensions between these parties over issues like information-sharing and other problems emerging from the interplay of states and markets. These disagreements, though, are often between players on the same side: government, industry and other stakeholders in any jurisdiction generally agree on the broad objectives. Their ambitions may diverge at times, as will their specific understandings of the purpose of cybersecurity, but they share the desire to improve national cybersecurity. You will hear these same governments articulate similar aspirations in the international arena too, at diplomatic summits and meetings of international organizations like the United Nations. However, because states see cyberspace as an environment in and through which to pursue their political and economic interests, they often disagree about its international rules, or indeed what cyberspace itself is for. As described in previous chapters, states and other actors use it for military and intelligence cyber operations against other countries, for commercial cyberespionage and a wide range of other cyber disruption. Importantly, it is also the platform for the surge in digital dis- and misinformation currently plaguing the global public sphere.[1] All of these activities affect international stability and security.

This chapter is about cyberspace as a competitive domain. Specifically, it looks at how states pursue their cybersecurity objectives in the international system, the effects of that on international security and stability, and how they seek to manage this situation. The first section looks at why countries use offensive cybersecurity as a tool of statecraft and its impacts on international security and stability. I then introduce the concept of global governance to describe the many programmes and initiatives that engage multiple stakeholders in addressing international cybersecurity problems, including offensive cybersecurity. The third section explores how major players contest the premises and ambitions of global cybersecurity governance and underlines that international cybersecurity is intensely geopolitical. The final section looks at states' disagreement over the applicability of international law to cybersecurity and to the specific lack of consensus on the central international political concept of sovereignty.

Offensive cybersecurity

Cyberspace is global. Although segments of the physical Internet are owned and operated by actors that identify with specific countries, these rarely map closely to national borders, even in countries that have tried to wall themselves off in some way from the global Internet, like China, Iran, Bahrain, Syria and Vietnam. To derive economic benefit from the Internet, any country must allow international data traffic across its borders so as to access global digital markets. The protocols of the global data environment, like TCP/IP and dozens of others, are shared by all; without them, there would be weakened security and no interoperability between networks. Despite their differences, countries are bound together by the protocols of cyberspace. Isolate yourself, and you will be unable to exploit cyberspace fully.

Exploitation is not limited to economic gain or general communications functions. National cybersecurity strategies make regular reference to leveraging the opportunities of global cyberspace for geostrategic purposes. These are usually couched in relatively neutral language. The UK, for instance, talks of 'operating in and through cyberspace to keep the country safe and to protect and promote the UK's interests at home and abroad.'[2] This mission statement, however, is in the context of describing its new National Cyber Force, set up in 2020 as a joint military-intelligence organization dedicated to offensive cyber (OC) for military, policing and counterterrorism operations.[3] Hypothetically, this is a legitimate use of sovereign capabilities, although there is no guarantee that all suitably equipped states will use OC responsibly. Experience shows that many do not. Additionally, exploitation requires knowledge of vulnerabilities. Should government agencies keep that knowledge to themselves, so they can use it for exploitation operations, or should they tell the wider cybersecurity community about these vulnerabilities, so that everyone can benefit from fixing them? Balancing these imperatives requires what is known as a vulnerabilities equities process (VEP), whereby each case is decided on its merits.[4] Critics argue that these processes are less than ideal and increase rather than reduce cyber risk. Given that we know hacking tools developed by intelligence agencies have ended up in the wrong hands, how can anyone be certain that their adversaries are not also in possession of that knowledge and poised to exploit it?[5] Vulnerabilities are at the core of cybersecurity and their exploitation always causes insecurity for someone or something.

At the systemic level, the types of operations enabled by exploiting vulnerabilities can, when perpetrated by states or proxy actors within their territory, contribute to international instability. Four factors are key. The first is that cyber capabilities are relatively cheap compared to most military and intelligence assets. This incentivizes states to develop them, although it remains difficult to develop the appropriate accompanying organizational infrastructures for cyber operations.[6] The second is that their use is easy to deny, which makes their deployment more attractive than conventional capabilities. Ones and zeroes are less easily traced to their origin than bombs and bullets. This is changing as attribution is becoming faster and more sophisticated, but most perpetrators of cyber operations deny their involvement.[7] Third, they can be used remotely without the need to deploy intelligence agents or troops abroad, thereby avoiding tricky political justifications for putting nationals in harm's way. These three factors are characteristics of cyberspace, but the fourth is geopolitical: the world is more unstable now than it has been for decades and states are looking for ways to achieve advantage in a turbulent international system. Cyberspace offers novel ways of doing this that are cheap, deniable and politically attractive. This has the net effect of increasing the worldwide proliferation of offensive cyber capabilities, contributing to international instability and undermining the peaceful use of cyberspace.

One of the truisms of international cybersecurity, therefore, is that there exists a permanent state of cyber conflict that decreases the overall level of security in the international system.[8] We have yet to see an all-out cyberwar, or a very large-scale warlike 'cyber attack', but all physical conflicts are now accompanied by cyber operations, such as Russia's war against Ukraine.[9] All ongoing inter-state disputes also have a cyber dimension, such as those between Israel and Iran, and India and Pakistan.[10] Persistent Chinese commercial cyberespionage against Western companies has demonstrably heightened geopolitical tensions, notably with the United States.[11] A generally conflictual relationship, unsurprisingly, also exists between cybercriminals and all those charged with defending digital systems or bringing criminals to justice. A long-standing concern is that cyber incidents could encourage conflict escalation, either from cyberspace to conventional engagements (vertical escalation), or by spilling out into the other military domains of land, sea, air and space or drawing in new participants (horizontal escalation).[12] This is fuelled by the difficulty of establishing an attacker's intentions, which could lead to wrongly calibrated responses, and by the possibility of collateral damage, given that cyber attacks can be difficult to control. So far, there is little hard data to support the escalation hypothesis, but there is abundant evidence that cyber operations foment inter-state mistrust and diplomatic tension below the threshold of war.

Global governance

Cybersecurity is a transnational concern and, like any other policy area with significant international implications – climate change, trade, intellectual property, communications – it requires structures and organizations that are not bound to the nation-state alone. Global governance emerged during the nineteenth century as a response to the rapid globalization of war, insecurity, capital and science and technology, particularly driven by European imperial expansion.[13] The central idea is that global governance allows transnational actors to make and enforce rules to solve global problems collectively in the absence of a world government. It is governance, not government. States are important players, but global governance also includes industry, civil society, expert communities, academia and non-governmental organizations. The international organizations and forums formed of these different groups are therefore multistakeholder (intergovernmental structures are known as multilateral).

The global governance of cybersecurity is complex. We have already encountered several examples of organizations involved in global governance, such as the technical expert communities that maintain global technical standards. The various information-sharing and cyber response teams that bridge the public and private sectors are grouped together in a global network, the Forum of Incident Response and Security Teams (FIRST), which develops global policy and standards in multistakeholder fashion.[14] Most of the companies with a stake in cybersecurity are either transnational in structure or sell into global markets; they are important voices in shaping global cybersecurity governance too. Microsoft, for example, has led the Cybersecurity Tech Accord, an industry initiative to protect their users from, among other things, state and state-sponsored cyber operations.[15] There is also a bewildering array of bespoke organizations contributing to cybersecurity governance in various ways. The Global Commission on the Stability of Cyberspace (GCSC), comprised largely of former ministers and officials, was active 2017–21 and explored ways to advance international security and stability in cyberspace.[16] The Global Cyber Alliance (GCA) is a non-profit organization that provides tools and resources to help reduce cyber risk.[17] The industry-led Charter of Trust aims 'to make the digital world of tomorrow a safer place'.[18] There are many more, as well as innumerable international conferences and forums that address cybersecurity issues with varying degrees of sophistication, resourcing and efficacy.

Almost all organizations with a transnational political remit also have a cybersecurity agenda. When we consider international organizations, the most prominent example is the United Nations (UN). Founded after the Second World War to enable international cooperation and foster peace and security, it has sponsored several initiatives with distinct importance for international cybersecurity. Some of these initiatives have been concerned with establishing frameworks for responsible state behaviour in cyberspace, including the acceptable use of offensive cyber operations. These involve developing and promoting cyber norms – shared beliefs about what states should and should not do in cyberspace – in the context of international peace and security. As we shall discuss further, these long-term processes have been convoluted and contested. The UN has a number of specialized agencies, one of which, the International Telecommunication Agency (ITU), is now part of the UN but was founded originally in 1865, during the first phase of global governance mentioned above. Since 2007 the ITU has had its own Global Cybersecurity Agenda, a 'framework for international cooperation aimed at enhancing confidence and security in the information society'.[19] Regional multilateral organizations like the African Union (AU), Association of Southeast Asian Nations (ASEAN) and European Union (EU) have also developed programmes that coordinate and harmonize their member-states' approaches to aspects of cybersecurity. Even an odd imperial remnant like the Commonwealth of Nations, mainly composed of former British colonies, has a Cyber Declaration Programme that promotes economic and social development through cybersecurity.[20]

The elevation of cybersecurity to an issue of global governance has necessitated the development of a new set of international political practices known as cyber diplomacy.[21] Diplomacy is the management of inter-state relations, usually through dialogue and negotiation conducted by professional diplomats. Its objectives are diverse but include the advancement of national interests through peaceful means and the maintenance of international peace and stability. Both objectives are important to cyber diplomacy, in which states pursue their own interests in cyberspace while respecting the collective cybersecurity aspirations of the international community. These are not necessarily mutually exclusive, but there are frequent tensions between diplomatic assertions of a state's probity and the reality of cyber statecraft in practice, and between blocs of states aligned with one vision of cybersecurity and those aligned with another.[22] Recent attention has been given to the promise of so-called Track 1.5 and Track 2 diplomacy, in which a wider group of stakeholders engages in 'quiet conversations' about cybersecurity on the margins of more formal diplomatic processes. Less constrained than official diplomats, participants can bring new issues to attention, develop novel cybersecurity solutions and feed back into higher-level cyber diplomacy.[23]

Despite its name, global governance is rarely completely global in scope or effect. To translate ideas and policy into collective action that achieves transnational cybersecurity goals, stakeholders must buy in to both the legitimacy of the various processes and the ambitions articulated. But in reality, they may refuse to engage with a particular institution or reject its proposals. It is also difficult to ensure appropriate implementation of policy and monitor, let alone enforce, compliance. The competitive nationalism of international affairs means that states prioritize their interests over those of the international community, often knowing that the penalties for breaches are weak or non-existent. Even where international law exists to regulate state behaviours, states can choose to break it and weather the subsequent diplomatic storm, public criticism and countermeasures, including sanctions. What is more likely, however, is that major players will contest the premises and content of proposed courses of action before anything concrete is agreed. The following section shows how this happens in international cybersecurity.

Contestation

Few states set out to deliberately undermine international peace and security. All commit – including through membership of the UN – to maintaining international stability. Predictability in international affairs means that states know what to expect from their friends as well as their foes, and how to pursue their interests within established rules of the game. The problem with international cybersecurity has long been knowing what those rules are, who sets them and what are the appropriate diplomatic venues in which to conduct these discussions. Since 2004 the UN Group of Governmental Experts (GGE) on information communications technologies (ICTs) and international security has attempted to work out some of these rules, principally in the form of norms for state behaviour in cyberspace. As noted previously, norms are shared beliefs about expected behaviour that states accept voluntarily. If everyone abides by them, they become strengthened and may eventually translate into international law and custom. If a country acts contrary to a norm, not only is that norm weakened but the offending party also risks ejection from the club of responsible states. Norms can therefore encourage positive behaviour in support of international cybersecurity and discourage behaviours that erode it. The challenge for the GGE was to develop a set of norms to which all state parties could agree, not an easy task given the divergent perceptions of the relationship between cyberspace and security.

The most influential states in the GGE disagreed on some fundamental issues. The United States – and its so-called 'like-minded' allies – have long promoted variations on an 'open, free, global, interoperable, reliable, and secure' Internet.[24] This political agenda covers a wide range of Internet issues from privacy and human rights to economic prosperity and a commitment to multistakeholder governance models. Russia, China and their strategic partners have consistently promoted a multilateral model that prioritizes the right of their governments to decide on cybersecurity and other issues, rather than deferring to a collective vision of cyberspace management. Insofar as they use the term cybersecurity at all, its main purpose is to secure the authority of their incumbent political regimes, not higher-level notions of international security. Russia and China prefer to speak of 'information security' that covers all uses of information within their borders. This is not the technical infosec described in Chapter 2 but a much wider concept of information control and authority that seeks to restrict political expression, digital mobilization and other forms of online activity that the regime considers potentially detrimental to its interests. They do not ignore cybersecurity altogether but reframe the relationship between cyberspace and security as primarily one of domestic information control for the purposes of regime security.

In foreign policy, these two visions are competitive and not easily reconcilable. They also affect far more than cybersecurity, with implications for human rights, industrial policy and trade. Despite these differences, the GGE managed over many years to develop four pillars and eleven norms for responsible state behaviour in cyberspace.[25] The pillars are: international law, the eleven voluntary norms, confidence-building measures (a form of inter-state trust-building diplomacy) and cybersecurity capacity-building as a category of development assistance (see Figure 4). The norms include peacetime obligations on states to work together to increase cyber stability; to not knowingly allow their territories to be used for cyberattacks; to share information on cyber threats and vulnerabilities; not to facilitate cyberattacks on critical infrastructures; to not harm CERTs and other incident response mechanisms; and other measures geared to improving overall levels of security and stability in cyberspace (see Figure 5). In 2021 these were endorsed by another UN process, the Open-Ended Working Group (OEWG) on information communications technologies (ICTs) and international security.[26] Whereas the GGE involved the permanent five members of the UN Security Council (China, France, Russia, UK, US) plus a rotating membership of roughly twenty others, the OEWG is open to all 193 members of the UN General Assembly and was deliberately designed to be more representative of the international community. The adoption of cyber principles and norms by all states is therefore

Figure 4: The four components of responsible state behaviour in cyberspace

INTERNATIONAL LAW
APPLIES TO STATE CONDUCT
IN CYBERSPACE

CYBER
CAPACITY
BUILDING
TO HARNESS
THE BENEFITS
AND MITIGATE
THE RISK OF
INCREASED
CONNECTIVITY

11 NORMS
SET CLEAR
EXPECTATIONS
OF
RESPONSIBLE
STATE
BEHAVIOUR
DURING
PEACETIME

CONFIDENCE-BUILDING MEASURES
STRENGTHENING TRANSPARENCY,
PREDICTABILITY AND STABILITY

an important step forward in developing a robust normative framework for international cybersecurity.

Norms do little work on their own: they need states to adopt, respect, promote and embed them in international practice. Global attention in the form of multilateral negotiations has therefore turned to the effective implementation of these cyber norms. This includes precisely what the norms mean in practice and whether states are complying with them. Arguably, one of the abiding behavioural norms is that many states openly articulate their respect for norms yet breach them in practice. The persistence

Figure 5: The eleven norms of responsible state behaviour in cyberspace

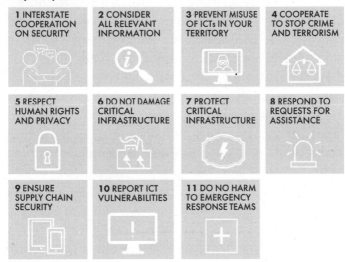

of Russian cyber operations against Western critical infrastructures, for instance, is in clear violation of the norms against misuse of ICTs and causing damage to critical infrastructure.[27] Some of these actions – and those by Iran, China and North Korea – have attracted sanctions by the US, EU and others, yet they continue with relative impunity.[28] China and Russia would counter by accusing the US and its allies of conducting offensive cyber operations of their own, often referring to historical activities revealed by Edward Snowden and ongoing unspecified cyber aggressions.[29] Albeit there is little evidence of the US attacking critical infrastructures, its strategic posture allows for operations in adversaries' cyberspace to deter cyber operations against the US or its allies.[30] The US and allies respond by asserting their adherence to the norms of responsible state behaviour developed at the UN and elsewhere, in contrast to the blatant breach of these norms by their strategic competitors. They also argue that their activities are in accordance with international law, one of the GGE's four principles. The next section explores disagreements over the applicability of international law to cybersecurity, paying particular attention to how governments interpret and use the central concept of sovereignty.

International law

As we have seen, the offensive use of cyber capabilities for strategic purposes is integrated in the overall concept of cybersecurity. In this register, a whole range of cyber activities is deployed to further the goals of national strategic and economic security, from digital intelligence and counterintelligence to cyberwarfare and counterterrorism. Governments can make the pragmatic case for their use, but are they permissible in international law? All 193 countries at the UN have endorsed a set of UN-brokered norms and principles. The latter include the understanding that international law, including the UN Charter, applies to state conduct in cyberspace. Quite how it applies is an area of ongoing state disagreement. One international legal concept in particular is subject to differing interpretations by states: sovereignty.

Sovereignty is a contested term in international law and practice anyway, but takes on new inflections in the context of ICTs and cybersecurity.[31] Some states argue that sovereignty is a rule of the international system, which, when coupled with assertions of inviolable territorial integrity, means that an external state's cyber actions against assets in another country are illegitimate, at least in peacetime. This is the position of countries like France and Brazil, who view any interference in their digital affairs as a breach of sovereignty. This includes gathering secret or confidential information through digital espionage, a practice that in its analogue form is not expressly prohibited under international law.[32] Other countries, notably the US and UK, regard sovereignty as a principle, a rather more flexible perspective in which sovereignty (and territory) are not absolute rights of the state. This would seem to permit – in their eyes – the use of cyber capabilities against another state should circumstances warrant it, such as the prevention of an imminent cyber attack or retaliation to existing digital aggression. Neither the GGE or OEWG has yet seemed keen to impose a definitive interpretation of sovereignty, with the situation remaining ambiguous and therefore permissive of cyber interventions in other states' affairs. Even allies like the members of NATO disagree on how sovereignty translates into the cyber domain and its resultant effects on the legitimacy of defensive and offensive cyber operations.[33]

The lack of consensus on the meaning of sovereignty has enabled another strand of state policy of relevance to cybersecurity. One interpretation of sovereignty implies that states have total authority over what happens within their territory, regardless of whether state actions respect international law and norms, such as those which uphold human rights. 'Cyber sovereignty' has emerged from China and Russia as a way of imposing territorial boundaries on cyberspace, within which the state decides what happens and why.[34] The transnational, networked nature of cyberspace means it is ill-suited to sovereignty that derives from viewing countries as physical, terrestrial entities.[35] This has not prevented countries from attempting to exert control over their 'national' internets, often framed as cybersecurity initiatives. The Cybersecurity Law of the People's Republic of China (2016) includes a wide range of reasonable provisions, many of which impose obligations on Internet service providers to improve cybersecurity and protect personal data. But it also locks the digital ecosystem into a national security framework, in which 'network operators', including social media platforms, must provide user data to the state in the service of vaguely defined national security requirements.[36] In China, national security is synonymous with regime security, so this type of cybersecurity legislation raises concerns about the human rights of Chinese citizens, or indeed anyone who wishes to do business in China. This fits a pattern of authoritarian regimes smuggling in repressive digital controls under the guise of cybersecurity.[37]

There are brighter spots in international cybersecurity law. A general consensus exists that the laws of armed conflict (international humanitarian law, IHL) apply to cyberspace, which means that military cyber operations in wartime must be necessary, proportionate and protect non-combatants to a high degree.[38] The Council of Europe has developed a Convention on Cybercrime (2001) to harmonize national cybercrime laws and develop law enforcement capacity.[39] Initially ratified by European countries, there are now over sixty-five parties to the 'Budapest Convention', from Chile to Senegal and Sri Lanka. In each of these cases, however, geopolitics intrudes. One leading opinion on IHL – the various iterations of the Tallinn Manual process – was rejected by Russia and China because that project was supported by NATO.[40] They have also rejected the applicability of IHL to cyberspace on the grounds that this would normalize it as a military domain, a disingenuous argument given that both countries regularly weaponize cyberspace this way.[41] Russia refuses to sign the Budapest Convention because the transnational policing cooperation it recommends would violate its sovereignty.[42] For many years, Brazil would not sign because of the convention's European origin; India continues its opposition on that basis.[43]

Like all law, international law is open to interpretation and, in the absence of a world court, it is governments in multilateral contexts that tend to decide what shape it should take. With respect to cybersecurity issues, this process is still at an early stage. While states debate the application of existing law, there is additional disagreement over whether new international law in the form of treaty mechanisms is required to address gaps and omissions. One commentator astutely described the various proposals as divided into treaties that 'protect states from people' and ones that 'protect people from states'.[44] In security terms, this is the difference between state/regime security and human security. Chinese and Russian treaty proposals fall into the first category.[45] Industry calls for a 'Digital Geneva Convention' align with the second.[46] In the absence of consensus on whether existing law is sufficient, what it looks like in practice and if new international law is required, the international law governing state cybersecurity practices will remain contested, fragmented and difficult to enforce.

Conclusion

The landscape of international cybersecurity is far from coherent. States disagree on the remit and aims of global cybersecurity governance, including norms and international law, as well as the forums in which global governance measures are developed. They also act in ways contrary to their declared diplomatic positions, an accusation that many would argue should not only be levelled at countries like Russia, China, Iran and North Korea. There is a sense in some quarters that the lack of an overarching binding and enforceable treaty that locks countries into a framework of responsible state behaviour in cyberspace means that global cybersecurity governance has failed. This argument requires us to accept that fragmentation in global governance is evidence of its inevitable collapse. This may be wrong, as no global governance regime is perfect, and all take time to be accepted and produce effects. We could perhaps flip the argument and ask what international cybersecurity would look like without global cyber norms and international law, however imperfect they may be. We should also accept that we are relatively early in this process, while recognizing that progress has been painfully slow at times. However, there is no doubt that the level of instability in the international system is increasing, and cybersecurity plays an important role in both elevating and dampening it. State use of offensive cyber operations and digital espionage may not be inherently escalatory, but it does little to foster good inter-state relations. Defensive cybersecurity can reduce opportunities for exploitation and deter malicious cyber operations. Norms can suggest what states should and should not do in this environment and law can deter bad actors further. It will require a lot more work by the global community to determine what works and what does not, a process that, in the absence of technical solutions, will be decided through intense multilateral and multistakeholder negotiation.

6
CYBERSECURITY AND HUMAN SECURITY

One of the foundational myths of cyberspace is that it promised a world beyond the state: a global communications space where people were free to explore their identities, build transnational communities and decide for themselves how cyberspace would evolve. Cyberlibertarian activist John Perry Barlow's famous 'Declaration of the Independence of Cyberspace', drafted on the fringes of the World Economic Forum in 1994, spoke directly to governments ('you weary giants of flesh and steel') when he told them, 'You are not welcome among us. You have no sovereignty where we gather.'[1]

Governments had other ideas, of course, and even the most ardent cyberlibertarians have long abandoned any pretence that cyberspace is somehow immune from state intervention or indeed from the sway of market forces. It is obvious that power and capital are propelling cybersecurity, particularly in its offensive dimensions, as much as the drive to defend computer networks and everything that depends on them. This should not be read as cynicism, but as an objective fact: national cybersecurity policies are just as clear about the exploitative opportunities of cyberspace as its potential to deliver social and economic benefits. The trick, if there is one, is to balance the needs and rights of individuals with the ambitions of national and international cybersecurity.

This chapter revisits some of the main themes of Chapters 3, 4 and 5 – risk, the state, international cybersecurity – but does so through the lens of individuals, rather than collective political units, firms and markets. It prioritizes individuals as the referents of cybersecurity, to use the term we explored in Chapter 3. The first section sets out human security as a useful vantage point from which to consider this shift in perspective and practice. Section two looks at cyber risk from this angle and considers the balance of cybersecurity responsibility between end-users and professionals. The third section explores some of the dynamics between citizens and the state, particularly how some countries use cybersecurity as a pretext for undermining individuals' security. It also asks about the central role of surveillance in technical cybersecurity. The final section looks at the human aspects of cyberwarfare and how states are trying to develop an ethical framework that preserves their ability to conduct cyberwarfare while respecting human security.

Human security

In Chapter 3, I offered a provisional definition of cybersecurity as the security one enjoys in, from and through cyberspace, and the measures taken to achieve this. This might seem quite broad, but it is consistent with national and international articulations of what cybersecurity is for. If we plug 'people' into this formulation, however, it helps us think more clearly about how we – citizens, civilians, end-users – can benefit from cybersecurity. A government spokesperson might say, 'Yes, that's great, but can you not see that our cybersecurity policies are inherently designed to protect and support your way of life? We've implemented numerous initiatives to ensure that you can safely navigate the Internet, free from cybercriminals and terrorists; what more do you want?' This is not unreasonable, and many countries have individually and collectively affirmed their commitment to put our cybersecurity at the heart of their ambitions and actions. As discussed in Chapter 5, though, cyberspace does not map easily to national territory and authority. It is transnational, which means that governments are limited in the resources they can bring to bear on cybersecurity problems and the global cyber threat landscape. Additionally, thinking about cybersecurity in parochially protective fashion ignores the insecurity that comes from exploiting cyberspace for strategic purposes, as in espionage and warfare, which might affect populations in other countries. It also fails to recognize the harms sometimes done in the name of cybersecurity, such as surveillance and repression.

'Human security' emerged in the 1990s as an approach to tackling global insecurity that put people first; in the jargon, it made them the primary referents of security. Specifically, it addressed the role of security in ensuring people's freedom from fear and want.[2] This agenda did not deny the importance of military action in responding to external aggression, but it did suggest that national interests might not always come before the wellbeing of civilians. Domestic and foreign policy should therefore be recalibrated to support human rights and development programmes that empowered people to determine their own futures and develop resilience to a wide range of non-military threats like disease, poverty and environmental degradation.[3] Importantly, human security was not just about ensuring people's basic survival in the face of threats; it emphasized that it was a way of meeting people's aspirations for a better life. As one influential scholar put it, 'Survival is being alive; security is living.'[4] Article 3 of the Universal Declaration of Human Rights (1948) states that, 'Everyone has the right to life, liberty and the security of person.' The state would act as a guarantor of this security, not as the objective of security in itself.

This is relevant to cybersecurity. If people don't come first – if they are not the primary referents of cybersecurity – what is the point of it? It cannot be the security of computer systems; this is meaningless outside the context of human action. If economic or national security are the aims of cybersecurity, how do they take account of people's wellbeing along the way? If regime security is the objective of cybersecurity in authoritarian countries, what rights are trampled or obscured to achieve it? While we can be relatively confident that most democratic countries act with probity and respect for human rights most of the time, this is not the universal situation. Nor does it excuse corporate and state practices anywhere that fail to meet legal, regulatory or normative obligations. We will look in more detail below at examples of how human security perspectives can help reframe key cybersecurity dynamics when it comes to the freedom from fear and want.

Freedom from fear suggests something else about cybersecurity that has long intrigued and annoyed observers. The language used by politicians, companies and the media to describe cyber threats has historically been bombastic and sometimes outright militaristic.[5] At times, it has played on well-known historical events, like Pearl Harbor and 9/11, to suggest that future cyber scenarios could have equally destructive effects on the social fabric and perhaps trigger significant state mobilization in response.[6] In one well-known book, a former White House official described in lurid detail how a cyber attack on the United States could cause chemical plants to explode and planes to fall from the sky, among other terrifying outcomes.[7] Frequently referencing cyberwar, these interventions are political and corporate marketing and often unhelpful. They are intended to raise decision-makers' awareness of cybersecurity issues, presumably followed by resource allocation, neither of which is inherently illegitimate, but the language of 'fear, uncertainty and doubt' (FUD) is a crude way of making one's case.[8] Importantly, it has tended to distract from the banal everyday of cybercrime and the rampant insecurity of hardware and software, each a more persistent problem than major cyber–physical attacks resulting in large-scale societal disruption. Arguing that something is possible is different from saying it is likely. It also means that one can never be wrong: a single future incident would justify all the rhetoric. As cybersecurity has been mainstreamed in national and international policy, the level of FUD has decreased recently, its marketing objectives largely met perhaps. Publics have also been very sceptical of cyber fearmongering, to their credit. It does suggest, though, that we need to talk about cybersecurity in careful language that communicates risk and threat in clear terms, shorn of hyperbole and fearful speculation.

Cyber risk

From the state or industry perspective, the main cause of cyber insecurity is often people. The cast list of miscreants is familiar, from hackers and hacktivists to insiders and terrorists, all of whom we can agree are baleful influences on cybersecurity. But there is another category of actor that poses a serious risk to cybersecurity: you. Perhaps you configured your firewall incorrectly and allowed your laptop to be harnessed in a botnet. Maybe you didn't have a firewall at all. Did you click on a bad link in an email and fail to notice that the website it took you to didn't look quite right? Maybe you replied to that official-looking message from Human Resources with the login details they requested so plausibly? Are your passwords on a sticky note on your monitor? Whatever happened, it was bad, and now someone has to clean up the mess. You are to blame. Or are you?

A top-down approach to cybersecurity will always try to offload blame on someone else. In the cybersecurity ecosystem, you and I are the end-users. We are at the edges of the network, tapping and swiping our devices with abandon, our insecure behaviours oblivious to a diverse and opportunistic threat landscape. No wonder we get blamed when things go wrong, even if we are usually the principal victims of cybercrime or other harms. There is some sense in this: we ignore security advice, snooze through our IT security briefing, do what we know we shouldn't, and expect someone else to clear up after us. We should all do better. But holding the end-user solely responsible is also profoundly misplaced. As the infosec thought leader Bruce Schneier has argued, this 'blame the victim' mentality is as wrong in cybersecurity as it would be in any other area of life. Stop trying to fix the user and fix the security instead.[9] If users are baffled or bored by constant prompts to do this or not to do that, it is the task of cybersecurity professionals to develop *usable* security that works for, rather than against us. Any other approach is a failure of leadership, not of the end-user.

We have to make decisions about risk every day and are not always best placed to determine the correct course of action. Cybersecurity looks like a field in which the profession should shoulder more of the burden. I ask my students who is responsible if a malicious email finds its way into their inbox. Answers range from the person who sent it to the systems administrators, Internet service provider and the email software itself. They rarely blame themselves. It may be that we don't handle malicious email in the best way, and possibly even suffer the consequences, but is it our fault it is there in the first place? No, it probably isn't. This does not mean that we should not be better aware and trained to cope with such things, but it does shift some of the responsibility back where it belongs: with professionals capable of making technical and organizational changes. Ideally, as Schneier argues, all of us should be pulling in the same direction, but blaming the end-user is a waste of time. Most infosec professionals know this and cybersecurity paradigms such as 'zero trust' emerge occasionally that promise new ways for users to interact securely with organizational networks and systems. Zero trust assumes that no user or device connected to a network can be trusted unless they can be properly authenticated at all times. All attempts to access an organization's applications and data need to be verified before access is granted; users and devices that fail these tests are blocked or required to verify their identity in other ways, thereby reducing the overall cyber risk to the enterprise. This need not be onerous to the user – and is highly automated anyway – but provides additional levels of security to organizations that, more than ever, work across multiple sites (including home and remote working) and with data stored both on-premises and in the cloud. You will also see organizations talk about 'layered security', which addresses aspects of a system or network architecture – servers, end-points, applications, data at rest and in transit – and protects against likely vectors of attack. 'Defence in depth' offers a wider range of security measures, including personnel and physical aspects, as advocated as far back as the 1970 Ware Report (Chapter 2). These measures cannot be perfect but, properly implemented, often together, they reduce the overall cyber risk to organizations and everything that depends on them.

From a human security perspective, they also reduce personal exposure to cyber risk. They cannot eradicate cyber threats, but they do minimize vulnerabilities. The personal impact of successful data breaches and cybercrimes is a different issue. It is sometimes overlooked in state-centric cybersecurity narratives that millions of people are defrauded by cybercriminals every year. In some countries, you are more likely to be the victim of cybercrime than any other type of crime. Even if it is an organization that is breached, there are potential human costs in lost revenue and redundancies. Should any countries experience large-scale outages of critical infrastructures as a result of hostile state or criminal cyber operations, it will be ordinary citizens who will suffer most, as it always is when governments and companies cannot deliver basic services.[10] The six-day fuel shortage caused by the Colonial Pipeline ransomware in 2021 is indicative in this respect. So too was a ransomware operation against a German hospital in 2020 that caused ambulances to be redirected elsewhere. A woman who died as a result of delayed treatment may have been the first death linked to a cyber attack.[11] In these circumstances, it is unrealistic to expect people to be resilient to events and dynamics wholly beyond their control, although, as indicated in Chapter 3, resilience is one of the standard approaches to cyber risk management.

Citizens and the state

A human security approach to the relationship between individuals and the state offers us the analogy of a house (the state) and its inhabitants (us).[12] What is the point of maintaining the fabric of the house and deterring intruders if the living conditions inside are poor? Moreover, what if the upkeep of the house costs so much that it reduces the wellbeing of the people living in it? This goes directly to the heart of what any form of security is for, cybersecurity included; none is an end in itself but must serve the interests of the people. There is, of course, great diversity in what constitutes a state, but those that consider themselves democratic and responsible understand that national security – and cybersecurity – provides for economic prosperity, societal stability and the possibilities of individual expression through leisure, education, employment and so on. States can meet the requirements of freedom from want by ensuring that cybersecurity is integral to the provision of public services and private goods, including critical infrastructures as diverse as healthcare, nuclear power, electricity, water, fuel, defence and the emergency services. This does not mean that these services are perfect – access to services is often discriminatory and poverty is a scourge of even the richest countries – but one of the principal aims of cybersecurity is to maintain what people need in their daily lives, as well as enable their aspirations and ambitions. Cybersecurity as national security can also be framed legitimately as furthering freedom from fear, although publics are becoming more aware than ever of the perils of transnational interconnectivity and the harm that can be caused through computer networks.

The security practices of states can also be compelling sources of individual insecurity. Where regime security, in particular, is prioritized over civil and human rights, governments cause insecurity through invidious military, law enforcement, judicial, counterterrorism and other security actions. If national security is the security of the nation, governments decide who should be treated as citizens and who discredited or dehumanized. The state observance of human security obligations collapses at this point, as fear and want are provoked and perhaps even encouraged. Cybersecurity might not seem an obvious vehicle for such outcomes, but two dynamics are worth bearing in mind.

The first is that governments do not all perceive cybersecurity alike. We have already encountered the idea that cybersecurity can be used to mask a range of state security practices that most countries would not consider as legitimate under the umbrella of cybersecurity. Countries like Egypt and some Gulf states deliberately introduce ambiguity into the meaning of cybersecurity that allows them to pursue domestic surveillance, the targeting of political opponents, and information controls.[13] At the same time, they shift the organizational centres of cybersecurity from technical expert communities like industry and academia deeper into the heart of the more conventional national security apparatus (policing, military, intelligence). This may appear duplicitous but is consistent with the definition of cybersecurity as the security one enjoys in, from and through cyberspace, and the measures taken to achieve this. Where it departs from more rights-respecting regimes is in prioritizing the state's security over the citizen's. Governments justify these measures in different ways. China stresses that cybersecurity should serve the interests of Chinese sovereignty and national goals of harmony, unity and stability. This seems reasonable until cybersecurity is subsumed within wider notions of information security that extend mass surveillance and information controls to all citizens, with particular attention paid to expressions of political and cultural identity that do not match those of Beijing. These may be domestic – Uighur, Falun Gong, Tibet, democracy – or wider 'Western' informational pollution, all of which are viewed as corrosive of Chinese stability, or, more accurately, the long-term survival of the Chinese Communist Party, which identifies itself as synonymous with both the state and the nation. This is an attractive model for other regimes to emulate, as China and Russia are keen to point out. Many Western states also exert some form of sovereignty over information flows, although they tend not to dress it up in the language of cybersecurity.[14]

The second relevant dynamic concerns how technical cybersecurity operates in practice. If you want to know what is happening on a given network or system, you need to monitor it and extract relevant data that you can use to inform decision-making. This is what all network security and other technical processes do at high-speed, at scale, and in automated fashion, often using artificial intelligence (machine learning) algorithms. This may not have the political charge of targeted surveillance of minorities or political opponents, but it is still a form of surveillance, not just of malware, cybercriminals and APTs but of user behaviours. We are told that 'surveillance is the business model of the Internet'.[15] Corporations provide services in exchange for our data, that are then commodified and used for a range of marketing purposes, giving rise to what has been called 'surveillance capitalism'.[16] The cybersecurity industry works on the same model and, although we should not leap to negative conclusions about the uses to which this data is put in everyday cybersecurity, we should remain mindful of what these technologies can do in the hands of government agencies. The Snowden disclosures suggest that mass collection of user data by democracies with the complicity of the private sector is real. The argument is not that cybersecurity surveillance is inherently invalid – it is not – but that it needs to be subject to oversight and accountability.

Ethics and cyber operations

Domestic cybersecurity is the main focus of most national cybersecurity policies. It is about securing cyberspace for economic prosperity and political stability, and to ensure the continued provision of essential goods and services to a country's citizens. As we have seen throughout previous chapters, cybersecurity is also used to promote national interests through interventions outside one's national borders. The two are intimately related. The defensive measures required to deter and counter APTs, foreign cybercriminals and other hostile actors are only necessary because other states conduct or condone these 'out of area' cyber operations. Much attention has been paid to Chinese commercial cyberespionage and Russian cyber disruption, but a host of other countries either have or are developing capabilities that allow them to conduct operations against other states for geostrategic purposes. This section looks at the human aspects of a subset of offensive cyber operations that is sometimes referred to as cyberwarfare. This is a contested term and for present purposes we will use it to refer to a form of military-intelligence statecraft that uses cyber capabilities to deny, disrupt, deceive, degrade or destroy the computerized assets or data of a foreign entity or state.[17] This implies an advanced state of hostilities between two or more countries, while excluding regular intelligence-gathering and espionage. This is of interest to us here because Western countries are developing an ethical framework for cyberwarfare that minimizes disruption to civilians, in accordance with international law and respect for human rights and security.

Cyberwarfare emerged in the 1990s as a new way of generating 'effect' in war.[18] Militaries speak of effect as the consequence of military (armed) and non-military actions. Military planners will therefore consider a range of physical, psychological, social or political effects that they desire, before deciding on which capabilities they need to deliver them. As countries became connected to the Internet, militaries too became more reliant on cyberspace for communications, command and control, presenting their adversaries with a greater potential 'attack surface' for the generation of effects that could turn a military confrontation in their favour. It also meant that civilian or non-military digital assets might be affected by military cyber operations, given the entanglement of civil and government networks. Under some circumstances, this could be unavoidable.

States considering cyber attacks against complex digital networks should understand and respect international humanitarian law (IHL) on the targeting of civilian infrastructures and its effect on non-combatants. IHL is clear that military operations should abide by the principles of necessity, distinction, proportionality and avoidance of unnecessary suffering. Cyber operations are also covered by these principles, meaning that attacks must be necessary to achieve military objectives, sufficiently distinguish between military and civilian targets, use no more force than is necessary, and minimize collateral civilian damage. There is a difference between knocking a radio station offline temporarily and permanently damaging a power grid, but each must consider whether it unduly affects civilians. This is relatively easy with kinetic (physical) attacks but is more complicated with cyber, which is harder to control and the effects of which are trickier to predict. Most cyberwarfare is non-lethal or reversible, so our notions of harm are different; it falls below the level of 'use of force' in a conventional sense. This may incentivize its use. Some have argued, for instance, that the use of cyber capabilities may be more ethical in war than alternative options.[19] However, it may be difficult to control the effects of cyber operations, given the interconnectedness of networks. Can you guarantee you have adhered to the principle of distinction if you cannot fully predict the consequences of a particular cyber operation? This is much easier to do with an airstrike or artillery, so may deter the use of cyber capabilities. How does one even judge the effects of a cyber operation? Conducting battle damage assessment is difficult for cyber, particularly when most of the effects are either informational or psychological, rather than physical. Cyberwarfare is therefore in something of a grey area relative to conventional military operations and there is significant discussion in defence circles of how to develop ethics for military cyber operations that uphold the principles of IHL, while permitting their use within defined constraints.[20]

This picture is complicated further by the rarity of conventional military confrontations. Most conflicts today are conducted between states and non-state actors – such as ISIS (Chapter 3) – or involve proxy forces that blur the line between combatant and civilian. This should not be interpreted as creating a permissive environment for cyberwarfare or any other form of offensive cybersecurity (although some countries conduct themselves as if it does). The US, for instance, has shown remarkable restraint in conducting offensive cyber operations in peace and war.[21] Contrary to popular belief perhaps, this suggests that countries like the US that have committed to upholding international law as part of responsible state behaviour in cyberspace (Chapter 5) extend this commitment to the use of cyberwarfare and other tools of offensive cybersecurity. One suggestion is that responsible cyber-capable states should develop a 'minimum effective offensive cyber capability', which would apply to all uses of offensive cyber, including cyberwarfare.[22] This would help abide by IHL and preserve the rights of civilians everywhere to security and liberty.

Conclusion

This chapter has proposed that we pay greater attention to the relationship between cybersecurity and human security. Cybersecurity has an important role in preserving human security, such as defending critical infrastructures from disruption and ensuring the delivery of key goods and services. It also needs to be communicated and managed in ways that encourage end-users to participate in the cybersecurity project. In its offensive register, cybersecurity can also undermine human security, such as through cyberwarfare, which is why responsible states are developing ethical frameworks that mitigate its negative effects. Elsewhere, cybersecurity is used as a cover for surveillance and political repression, with resultant erosion of human security and human rights. We all need to be attentive to these dynamics and address them where we can, pressing our governments to uphold the normative and legal regimes to which they have committed, as described in Chapter 5.

If it seems that we have moved far from technical cybersecurity, it is because we have. This book argues that cybersecurity – in the round – is a political project. It is the object of national and international policy, of law, regulation and global governance. Its priorities and objectives are decided and implemented by the high politics of states and the everyday politics of stakeholders across technical communities, academia and civil society. In the Conclusion that follows, I will tie together some of the themes developed in this book and offer some thoughts for taking cybersecurity forward into the twenty-first century.

7

CONCLUSION: A GLOBAL CONVERSATION

The aim of this book is to provide readers with tools for understanding cybersecurity and its role in the contemporary world. I have suggested that we need to think about cybersecurity as a complex interplay of people and technologies, rather than as a purely technical field reserved for computer scientists and cybersecurity professionals. Cybersecurity touches all areas of life, such is the intensity and scale of digital transformation. If cybersecurity is a 'wicked problem', it cannot be solved through science and technology alone. It needs people from a wide range of backgrounds and specialisms to contribute to a global conversation about how to secure our digital world from the many threats posed to it from deliberate and accidental disruption. The central proposition threaded through the chapters is that cybersecurity is political, at every level from the technical to the national and international.

Chapter 2 provided an account of how cybersecurity emerged in the late twentieth century from earlier formulations of information security. This occurred because computer systems came out of the university and laboratory and became the connective fibre of global commerce and communications. The Internet is possibly the most transformative technology in human history, but it brought with it vulnerabilities that once embedded into socioeconomic systems became ripe for exploitation by criminals, hackers and hostile states. Our dependence on cyberspace has become our vulnerability, one that has no technical fix.

Chapter 3 addressed the cyber threat landscape in more detail, particularly criminal and political threats, and how cyber risk management and resilience have developed to tackle the overall cyber threat to individuals, firms, states and international order. This allowed us to see that cybersecurity intends to secure a range of different objects, known as 'security referents'. At this point, we were able to introduce a provisional definition of cybersecurity as the security one enjoys in, from and through cyberspace, and the measures taken to achieve this. Cybersecurity is both a desirable condition and the journey we take to get there.

Chapter 4 illustrated how cybersecurity takes place in the interaction of the public and private sectors, each of which takes a different approach to what it hopes to gain from cybersecurity. The tensions between public service and profit motives can sometimes be mitigated through organizational arrangements like public–private partnerships but nevertheless persist. At times, we must wonder whose ambitions are being served by cybersecurity and this chapter drew attention to some of its darker aspects. So too did Chapter 5, although the main attention here was on the contestation of political visions of what cyberspace and cybersecurity should look like in the international system. This is cybersecurity as a tool and function of competing geopolitical agendas and as a challenge to international security and stability.

This book asks the question, 'What is cybersecurity for?', and Chapter 6 answered that, ultimately, cybersecurity is for us. Through the lens of human security, cybersecurity should ensure freedom from fear and want, as should any form of security, military or otherwise. This does not mean that cybersecurity should not also be for technical, national, economic or international security – it should, and it would be nonsensical to claim otherwise. Like a house and its inhabitants, the state and international community are well placed to provide the cybersecurity shelter within which we can be secure and thrive. The private sector can help with the upkeep of this edifice (for a fee, of course), but human security should be paramount. When we look at some forms of offensive cybersecurity or digital espionage, for instance, we must develop frameworks for their use that prioritize human rights and security while achieving national and international security objectives. This will always be a difficult task in a world that is backsliding into competitive nationalism and increasingly sees 'cyber' as a domain to exploit in the national interest. States have agreed a normative framework for responsible state behaviour in cyberspace, including upholding the international law that can guarantee human security objectives, but their actions frequently undermine it. The cyber threat landscape is evolving fast too, as the global attack surface grows with an insecure IoT as digital transformation continues apace, and as attackers turn to artificial intelligence and other innovations to effect data breaches, critical infrastructure disruption and supply chain attacks. The next decade is likely to see levels of cyber insecurity rise not fall.

Cybersecurity is an essential dimension of the contemporary world. Without it, the global digital transformation that has been under way in recent decades would likely collapse under the weight of its inherent flaws and insecure design. Managing cyber risk is necessary in order for everyone to benefit from the global information environment. This cannot be just a technical project, as I hope to have established in this book. Cybersecurity practitioners, software and hardware designers, network engineers and computer scientists of every stripe are crucial partners in developing cybersecurity solutions, but not all solutions can be developed in the technical realm. Global cyberspace is seen by states, criminals, hacktivists, terrorists and others as open to exploitation for strategic and financial gain. States and their proxies are finding new avenues for competition, often acting brazenly and with impunity, threatening international security and stability as they do. These problems need political resolution and, despite robust international efforts to coordinate such activities, there are no guarantees that consensual and effective approaches will be achieved.

This message is not a counsel of despair, despite its pessimistic overtones. It is surely, though, what the cybersecurity community often describes as a wake-up call. However we understand cybersecurity and its principal functions, we should contextualize it within the troubled landscape of digital technologies, one beset by the 'intertwined pathologies' of digital repression, corporate surveillance, state exploitation and rampant consumerism.[1] This book has not attempted to tackle the pernicious effects of information warfare, for instance, which attempts to exploit social divisions and thereby undermine social cohesion and trust in democratic institutions. It is tempting to identify crude human nature as the debilitating cause of this general malaise, until we remember that most people are not the cybersecurity problem: the few cause problems for the many. It may be that restoring human security to the centre of all technology and public policy is – realistically – the only sensible way forwards. No other approaches have yet worked, although we should not underestimate how much progress has been made in some quarters in raising awareness if not in finding lasting solutions.

I said in the Introduction that I had no intention of trying to 'solve' cybersecurity. I do genuinely believe, however, that rebalancing the competing securities of cybersecurity is necessary. If cybersecurity is not serving the interests of diverse humanity, it is not acting as it should. This means cybersecurity in its defensive and offensive forms must put people first. States and firms are crucial enablers of cybersecurity, often because they are the entities that make things happen, drive policy and innovation, and develop rules and guidelines that constrain and incentivize cybersecurity. States and firms need to find ways to build human needs and concerns into cybersecurity from the ground up, whether in product design, service provision, policy development or political decision-making. Their activities should also be subject to increased accountability, not least so as to avoid 'mission creep' or 'function creep'. (Mission creep refers to the expansion of an initiative or policy beyond its original focus, function (or scope) creep to the use of information or technology beyond its originally specified purpose.) We have seen both regularly in cybersecurity and the wider use of technologies, particularly in the rolling-up of policing online content and expression in the name of cybersecurity.

States, in particular, need to develop cooperative modes that reduce conflict and tension at home and abroad. This does not necessarily imply a 'one size fits all' cybersecurity solution. Local and regional preferences must be respected, particularly in the Global South, where countries do not necessarily wish to adopt edicts handed down by the great powers. This again underscores the importance of democratic multilateral deliberation and the centrality of multistakeholder communities. Under conditions of intensifying international competition, however, cybersecurity is likely to promote national security at the expense of human security; we need to address the structural conditions of cyberspace that incentivize this imbalance. Defensive cybersecurity can play a significant role in that by deterring threats and reducing vulnerabilities. Unfortunately, the exploitation of cyberspace by 'bad' and 'good' actors (who decides which is which?) means that military, intelligence and law enforcement must continue to tackle them, but we should be alert to the counterproductive effects of some of their actions, particularly when spurred on by states that care little for international order and the rule of law.

Cybersecurity is a vast field of theory and practice that affects every element of society, economics, politics and human interaction. In this short book I have introduced some key ideas that I hope will encourage reflection on its more problematic aspects. If it has raised readers' awareness of the cybersecurity challenge, it will have achieved its primary objective. If it prompts you to join the conversation, so much the better.

NOTES

Chapter 1

1   National Audit Office (2018) *Investigation: WannaCry Cyber Attack and the NHS*, 25 April 2018, https://www.nao.org.uk/wp-content/uploads/2017/10/Investigation-WannaCry-cyber-attack-and-the-NHS-Summary.pdf.

2   Jonathan Berr, 'WannaCry Ransomware Attack Losses Could Reach $4bn', *CBS News*, 16 May 2017, https://www.cbsnews.com/news/wannacry-ransomware-attacks-wannacry-virus-losses/.

3   Eric S. Raymond, *The Cathedral and the Bazaar: Musings on Linux and Open Source by an Accidental Revolutionary* (O'Reilly Media, 2008), p. 30.

4   National Cyber Security Centre and KPMG UK, *Decrypting Diversity: Diversity and Inclusion in Cyber Security*, 2020, https://www.ncsc.gov.uk/files/Decrypting-Diversity-v1.pdf.

Chapter 2

1   Norbert Wiener, *Cybernetics: Or, Control and Communication in the Animal and the Machine* (Technology Press, 1949).

2   David Alan Grier, *When Computers Were Human* (Princeton University Press, 2005).

3   Christopher Hollings, Ursula Martin and Adrian Rice, 'How Ada Lovelace's Notes on the Analytical Engine Created the First Computer Program', *BBC Science Focus Magazine*, 13 October 2020, https://www.sciencefocus.com/future-technology/how-ada-lovelaces-notes-on-the-analytical-engine-created-the-first-computer-program/.

4   Paul E. Ceruzzi, *A History of Modern Computing* (second edition, MIT Press, 2003).

5   RAND Corporation, *Security Controls for Computer Systems: Report of Defense Science Board Task Force on Computer Security*, 11 February 1970, https://csrc.nist.gov/csrc/media/publications/

conference-paper/1998/10/08/proceedings-of-the-21st-nissc-1998/
documents/early-cs-papers/ware70.pdf.

6. RAND Corporation, *Security Controls*, p. vi.

7. HM Government, *National Cyber Strategy 2022: Pioneering a Cyber Future with the Whole of the UK*, 15 December 2021. https://www.gov.uk/government/publications/national-cyber-strategy-2022.

8. Cade Metz, 'Paul Baran, the Link between Nuclear War and the Internet', *Wired*, 9 April 2012, https://www.wired.co.uk/article/h-bomb-and-the-internet.

9. Giovanni Navarria, 'How the Internet was Born: From the ARPANET to the Internet', *The Conversation*, 2 November 2016, https://theconversation.com/how-the-internet-was-born-from-the-arpanet-to-the-internet-68072.

10. Finn Brunton, *Spam: A Shadow History of the Internet* (MIT Press, 2013).

11. Steven Levy, *Hackers: Heroes of the Computer Revolution* (O'Reilly, 2010).

12. Jussi Parikka, *Digital Contagions: A Media Archaeology of Computer Viruses* (Peter Lang, 2016).

13. FBI, 'Morris Worm', https://www.fbi.gov/history/famous-cases/morris-worm.

14. Cliff Stoll, *The Cuckoo's Egg* (Pocket Books, 1990).

15. Juan Andres Guerrero-Saade, Daniel Moore, Costin Raiu and Thomas Rid, *Penquin's Moonlit Maze: The Dawn of Nation-State Digital Espionage*, 3 April 2017, https://media.kasperskycontenthub.com/wp-content/uploads/sites/43/2018/03/07180251/Penquins_Moonlit_Maze_PDF_eng.pdf.

16. National Security Archive, 'Eligible Receiver 97: Seminal DOD Cyber Exercise Included Mock Terror Strikes and Hostage Simulations', 1 August 2018, https://nsarchive.gwu.edu/briefing-book/cyber-vault/2018-08-01/eligible-receiver-97-seminal-dod-cyber-exercise-included-mock-terror-strikes-hostage-simulations.

17. Nathan Thornburgh, 'The Invasion of the Chinese Cyberspies', *Time*, 29 August 2005, https://content.time.com/time/subscriber/article/0,33009,1098961,00.html.

18. Ellen Messmer, 'Kosovo Cyber-war Intensifies: Chinese Hackers Targeting US Sites, Government Says', CNN, 12 May 1999, http://edition.cnn.com/TECH/computing/9905/12/cyberwar.idg/.

19. C.M. Wade, 'Chinese Hackers Threaten May Day Attack', UPI, 27 April 2001, https://www.upi.com/Archives/2001/04/27/Chinese-hackers-threaten-May-Day-attack/8929988344000/.

20   James Glave, 'Crackers: We Stole Nuke Data', *Wired*, 3 June 1998, https://www.wired.com/1998/06/crackers-we-stole-nuke-data/.

21   Niall McKay, 'China: The Great Firewall', *Wired*, 1 December 1998, https://www.wired.com/1998/12/china-the-great-firewall/.

22   FBI, 'A Byte Out of History: $10 Million Hack, 1994-style', 31 January 2014, https://www.fbi.gov/news/stories/a-byte-out-of-history-10-million-hack.

23   European Commission, *On a European Programme for Critical Infrastructure Protection*, 17 November 2005, https://eur-lex.europa.eu/LexUriServ/LexUriServ.do?uri=COM:2005:0576:FIN:EN:PDF.

24   National Cyber Security Centre, 'Operational Technologies', 6 February 2017, https://www.ncsc.gov.uk/guidance/operational-technologies.

25   Lily Hay Newman, 'Colonial Pipeline Paid a $5M Ransom – and Kept a Vicious Cycle Turning', *Wired*, 14 May 2021, https://www.wired.com/story/colonial-pipeline-ransomware-payment/.

26   Ben Buchanan, *The Cybersecurity Dilemma: Hacking, Trust, and Fear Between Nations* (Hurst, 2016).

27   Jason Jaskoika, 'Cyberattacks to Critical Infrastructure Threaten Our Safety and Well-Being', *The Conversation*, 24 October 2021, https://theconversation.com/cyberattacks-to-critical-infrastructure-threaten-our-safety-and-well-being-170191.

28   Craig Barber, 'Global Internet Outages Explained', British Computer Society, 14 December 2021, https://www.bcs.org/articles-opinion-and-research/global-internet-outages-explained/.

Chapter 3

1   Jonathan Lusthaus, *Industry of Anonymity: Inside the Business of Cybercrime* (Harvard University Press, 2018).

2   Kurt Baker, 'Ransomware as a Service (RaaS) Explained', Crowdstrike, 7 February 2022, https://www.crowdstrike.com/cybersecurity-101/ransomware/ransomware-as-a-service-raas/.

3   Sophos, *The State of Ransomware in Education 2022*. July 2022, https://assets.sophos.com/X24WTUEQ/at/pgvqxjrfq4kf7njrncc7b9jp/sophos-state-of-ransomware-education-2022-wp.pdf.

4   Leigh McGowan, 'Ransomware Attack Forces French Hospital to Transfer Patients', *Silicon Republic*, 25 August 2022, https://www.siliconrepublic.com/enterprise/ransomware-cyberattack-french-hospital-chsf.

5   Kevin Collier, 'Cyberattacks against US hospitals mean higher mortality rates, study finds', *NBS News*, 8 September 2022, https://www.nbcnews.com/tech/security/cyberattacks-us-hospitals-mean-higher-mortality-rates-study-finds-rcna46697.

6   Cisco, 'What is a Social Engineering Attack?', https://www.cisco.com/c/en_uk/products/security/what-is-social-engineering.html.

7   Martin C. Libicki, *Cyberdeterrence and Cyberwar* (RAND Corporation, 2009), p. xiv.

8   Lily Hay Newman, 'A Year After the SolarWinds Hack, Supply Chain Threats Still Loom', *Wired*, 8 December 2021, https://www.wired.com/story/solarwinds-hack-supply-chain-threats-improvements/.

9   Tim Stevens, 'Strategic Cyberterrorism: Problems of Ends, Ways and Means', 2019, https://papers.ssrn.com/sol3/papers.cfm?abstract_id=4031628.

10 Symantec, 'Dragonfly: Western Energy Sector Targeted by Sophisticated Attack Group', 20 October 2017, https://symantec-enterprise-blogs.security.com/blogs/threat-intelligence/dragonfly-energy-sector-cyber-attacks.

11 Laura Dobberstein, 'Beijing-Backed Attackers Use Ransomware as a Decoy While They Conduct Espionage', *The Register*, 24 June 2022, https://www.theregister.com/2022/06/24/ransomware_as_espionage_distraction/.

12 'Operating Glowing Symphony (2016)', https://cyberlaw.ccdcoe.org/wiki/Operation_Glowing_Symphony_(2016).

13 Mandiant, *APT1: Exposing One of China's Cyber Espionage Units*, February 2013, https://www.mandiant.com/sites/default/files/2021-09/mandiant-apt1-report.pdf.

14 Taylor Armerding, 'Chinese Army Link to Hack No Reason for Cyberwar', *CSO*, 19 February 2013, https://www.csoonline.com/article/2133010/chinese-army-link-to-hack-no-reason-for-cyberwar.html.

15 Kurt Baker, 'What Is Cyber Threat Intelligence?', Crowdstrike, 17 March 2022, https://www.crowdstrike.com/cybersecurity-101/threat-intelligence/.

16 BBC, 'The Lazarus Heist: How North Korea Almost Pulled Off a Billion-Dollar Hack', 21 June 2021, https://www.bbc.co.uk/news/stories-57520169.

17 Teyloure Ring, 'Rank and File Corrupted: Uncertain Attribution and Corruption in Russia's Military Cyber Units', Center for Strategic and International Studies, 22 September 2020,

https://www.csis.org/blogs/post-soviet-post/rank-and-file-corrupted-uncertain-attribution-and-corruption-russias-military.

18 Tim Maurer, *Cyber Mercenaries: The State, Hackers, and Power* (Cambridge University Press, 2018).

19 Rupert Jones, 'Fraud in UK at Level Where It "Poses National Security Threat"', *Guardian*, 22 September 2001, https://www.theguardian.com/money/2021/sep/22/fraud-in-uk-at-level-poses-national-security-threat-bank-customers-covid.

20 Aaron Gregg, Sean Sullivan and Stephanie Hunt, 'As Colonial Pipeline Recovers from Cyberattack, Leaders Point to a "Wake-Up" Call for US Energy Infrastructure', *Washington Post*, 13 May 2021.

21 Joe Devanny, Ciaran Martin and Tim Stevens, 'On the Strategic Consequences of Digital Espionage', *Journal of Cyber Policy*, 6 (2021), pp. 429–50, https://www.tandfonline.com/doi/full/10.1080/23738871.2021.2000628.

22 Gregory Falco and Eric Rosenbach, *Confronting Cyber Risk* (Oxford University Press, 2022), pp. 79–86.

23 Ursula von der Leyen, 'State of the Union Address', 15 September 2021, https://ec.europa.eu/commission/presscorner/detail/en/SPEECH_21_4701.

24 David Forscey, Jon Bateman, Nick Beecroft and Beau Woods, *Systemic Cyber Risk: A Primer*, 7 March 2022, Carnegie Endowment for International Peace, https://carnegieendowment.org/2022/03/07/systemic-cyber-risk-primer-pub-86531.

25 J.R. Minkel, 'The 2003 Northeast Blackout – Five Years Later', *Scientific American*, 13 August 2008, https://www.scientificamerican.com/article/2003-blackout-five-years-later/.

26 Josh Taylor, 'Facebook Outage: What Went Wrong and Why Did It Take So Long to Fix After Social Platform Went Down?', *Guardian*, 5 October 2021, https://www.theguardian.com/technology/2021/oct/05/facebook-outage-what-went-wrong-and-why-did-it-take-so-long-to-fix.

27 Matt Burgess, 'What Is the Internet of Things? WIRED Explains', *Wired*, 16 February 2018, https://www.wired.co.uk/article/internet-of-things-what-is-explained-iot.

Chapter 4

1 International Telecommunications Union, 'National Cybersecurity Strategies Repository', https://www.itu.int/en/ITU-D/Cybersecurity/Pages/National-Strategies-repository.aspx.

2   Global Cyber Security Capacity Centre, 'Cybersecurity Capacity Maturity Model', https://gcscc.ox.ac.uk/the-cmm.

3   Louise Marie Hurel, *Cybersecurity in Brazil: An Analysis of the National Strategy* (Igarapé Institute, April 2021), https://igarape.org.br/wp-content/uploads/2021/04/SP-54_Cybersecurity-in-Brazil.pdf.

4   HM Government, *National Cyber Strategy 2022: Pioneering a Cyber Future with the Whole of the UK*, 15 December 2021, https://www.gov.uk/government/publications/national-cyber-strategy-2022.

5   Ryan Singel, 'Cyberwar Hype Intended to Destroy the Open Internet', *Wired*, 1 March 2010, https://www.wired.com/2010/03/cyber-war-hype/.

6   https://www.submarinecablemap.com/

7   Nicky Woolf, 'DDoS Attack that Disrupted Internet Was Largest of Its Kind in History, Experts Say', *Guardian*, 26 October 2016, https://www.theguardian.com/technology/2016/oct/26/ddos-attack-dyn-mirai-botnet.

8   Graham Cluley, 'Did the Mirai Botnet Knock Liberia Offline? Not So Much', 6 November 2016, https://grahamcluley.com/did-mirai-botnet-liberia-offline/.

9   HM Government, *National Cyber Security Strategy 2016–2021*, November 2016, p. 9, https://www.gov.uk/government/publications/national-cyber-security-strategy-2016-to-2021.

10   James Coker, 'UK Introduces New Cybersecurity Legislation for IoT Devices', *Infosecurity Magazine*, 24 November 2021, https://www.infosecurity-magazine.com/news/uk-cybersecurity-legislation-iot/.

11   ENISA, *Cybersecurity as an Economic Enabler*, March 2016, https://www.enisa.europa.eu/publications/enisa-position-papers-and-opinions/cybersecurity-as-an-economic-enabler.

12   National Cyber Security Centre, 'Penetration Testing', 8 August 2017, https://www.ncsc.gov.uk/guidance/penetration-testing.

13   Amitai Etzioni, 'Cybersecurity in the Private Sector', *Issues in Science and Technology* 28 (2011), https://issues.org/etzioni-2-cybersecurity-private-sector-businesses/.

14   Greg Austin, *Cyber Policy in China* (Wiley, 2014).

15   Madeline Carr, 'Public-Private Partnerships in National Cyber-Security Strategies', *International Affairs* 92 (2016), pp. 43–62, https://www.chathamhouse.org/sites/default/files/publications/ia/INTA92_1_03_Carr.pdf.

16   Republic of Estonia, 'Information System Authority', https://www.
      ria.ee/en.html.

17   ENISA, *Public Private Partnerships (PPP): Cooperative Models*,
      November 2017, https://www.enisa.europa.eu/publications/public-
      private-partnerships-ppp-cooperative-models.

18   National Cyber Security Centre, 'Industry 100: About', https://
      www.ncsc.gov.uk/section/industry-100/about.

19   Jamie Collier, 'Optimising Cyber Security Public-Private
      Partnerships', *RUSI Commentary*, 28 May 2021, https://rusi.org/
      explore-our-research/publications/commentary/optimising-cyber-
      security-public-private-partnerships.

20   Hugo Rosemont, *Public–Private Security Cooperation: From
      Cyber to Financial Crime*, RUSI Occasional Paper, August 2016,
      https://rusi.org/explore-our-research/publications/occasional-papers/
      public-private-security-cooperation-cyber-financial-crime.

21   ENISA, *Information Sharing and Analysis Centres (ISACs):
      Cooperative Models*, February 2018, https://www.enisa.europa.
      eu/publications/information-sharing-and-analysis-center-isacs-
      cooperative-models.

22   Brendan I. Koerner, 'Inside the Cyberattack That Shocked the
      US Government', *Wired*, 23 October 2016, https://www.wired.
      com/2016/10/inside-cyberattack-shocked-us-government/.

23   HM Government, *National Cyber Strategy 2022*, p. 8.

24   David Talbot, 'The Cyber Security Industrial Complex',
      MIT Technology Review, 6 December 2011, https://www.
      technologyreview.com/2011/12/06/189326/the-cyber-security-
      industrial-complex/.

25   Benjamin Verdi, 'The Coming Cyber-Industrial Complex: A
      Warning for the New US Administration', *Geopolitical Monitor*,
      22 November 2020, https://www.geopoliticalmonitor.com/the-
      coming-cyber-industrial-complex-a-warning-for-the-new-us-
      administration/.

26   James Shires, *The Politics of Cybersecurity in the Middle East*
      (Hurst, 2021).

27   Bill Marczak, John Scott-Railton, Sarah McKune, Bahr Abdul
      Razzak and Ron Deibert, 'Hide and Seek: Tracking NSO Group's
      Pegasus Spyware to Operations in 45 Countries', *Citizen Lab*,
      18 September 2018, https://citizenlab.ca/2018/09/hide-and-
      seek-tracking-nso-groups-pegasus-spyware-to-operations-in-45-
      countries/.

28 Nicole Perlroth, *This Is How They Tell Me the World Ends: The Cyber Weapons Arms Race* (Bloomsbury, 2021).

29 Lillian Ablon, Martin C. Libicki and Andrea A. Golay, *Markets for Cybercrime Tools and Stolen Data: Hackers' Bazaar* (RAND Corporation, 2014), https://www.rand.org/pubs/research_reports/RR610.html.

30 Sydney Lake, 'Companies are Desperate for Cybersecurity Workers – More Than 700k Positions Need to Be Filled', *Fortune*, 30 June 2022, https://fortune.com/education/business/articles/2022/06/30/companies-are-desperate-for-cybersecurity-workers-more-than-700k-positions-need-to-be-filled/.

31 Tommaso De Zan, 'The Strategic Relevance of Cybersecurity Skills', *Lawfare*, 27 June 2022, https://www.lawfareblog.com/strategic-relevance-cybersecurity-skills.

32 Florian J. Egloff, *Semi-State Actors in Cybersecurity* (Oxford University Press, 2022).

Chapter 5

1 Christopher Whyte, A. Trevor Thrall and Brian M. Mazanec (eds.), *Information Warfare in the Age of Cyber Conflict* (Routledge, 2021).

2 HM Government, *National Cyber Strategy 2022: Pioneering a Cyber Future for the Whole of the UK*, 15 December 2021, p. 24, https://www.gov.uk/government/publications/national-cyber-strategy-2022.

3 Joe Devanny, Andrew Dwyer, Amy Ertan and Tim Stevens, *The National Cyber Force That Britain Needs?* (King's Policy Institute, April 2021), https://www.kcl.ac.uk/policy-institute/research-analysis/national-cyber-force.

4 Nicholas Weaver, 'The GCHQ's Vulnerabilities Equities Process', *Lawfare*, 3 June 2019, https://www.lawfareblog.com/gchqs-vulnerabilities-equities-process.

5 Andi Wilson Thompson, 'Assessing the Vulnerabilities Equities Process, Three Years After the VEP Charter', *Lawfare*, 13 January 2021, https://www.lawfareblog.com/assessing-vulnerabilities-equities-process-three-years-after-vep-charter.

6 Max Smeets, *No Shortcuts: Why States Struggle to Develop a Military Cyber-Force* (Hurst, 2022).

7 Clement Guitton, *Inside the Enemy's Computer: Identifying Cyber-Attackers* (Hurst, 2017).

8   Patryk Pawlak, Eneken Tikk and Mike Kerttunen, *Cyber Conflict Uncoded: The EU and Conflict Prevention in Cyberspace* (European Union Institute for Security Studies, 17 April 2020), https://www.iss.europa.eu/content/cyber-conflict-uncoded.

9   Monica Kaminska, James Shires and Max Smeets, *Cyber Operations during the 2022 Russian Invasion of Ukraine: Lessons Learned (So Far)* (European Cyber Conflict Research Initiative, July 2022), https://doi.org/10.3929/ethz-b-000560503.

10   Joe Tidy, 'Predatory Sparrow: Who are the Hackers Who Say They Started a Fire in Iran?', BBC News, 11 July 2022, https://www.bbc.co.uk/news/technology-62072480.

11   Huileng Tan, 'China Sees Cyber Espionage as a "Necessary" Part of Its National Strategy, Expert Says', CNBC, 21 December 2018, https://www.cnbc.com/2018/12/21/doj-accuses-china-of-hacking-.html.

12   Martin C. Libicki and Olesya Tkacheva, 'Cyberspace Escalation: Ladders or Lattices', in Ertan, Floyd, Pernik and Stevens (eds.), *Cyber Threats and NATO 2030: Horizon Scanning and Analysis* (NATO CCD COE, 2020), pp. 60–72, https://ccdcoe.org/library/publications/cyber-threats-and-nato-2030-horizon-scanning-and-analysis/.

13   Mark Mazower, *Governing the World: The History of an Idea* (Penguin, 2012).

14   https://www.first.org/

15   https://cybertechaccord.org/accord/

16   GCSC, *Advancing Cyberstability: Final Report*, November 2019, https://cyberstability.org/report/.

17   https://www.globalcyberalliance.org/

18   https://www.charteroftrust.com/

19   https://www.itu.int/en/action/cybersecurity/Pages/gca.aspx

20   'Commonwealth Cyber Declaration Programme', https://thecommonwealth.org/our-work/commonwealth-cyber-declaration-programme.

21   Cristin J. Monahan, 'A Diplomatic Domain? The Evolution of Diplomacy in Cyberspace', National Security Archive, 26 April 2021, https://nsarchive.gwu.edu/briefing-book/cyber-vault/2021-04-26/diplomatic-domain-evolution-diplomacy-cyberspace.

22   Kieron O'Hara and Wendy Hall, *Four Internets: Data, Geopolitics, and the Governance of Cyberspace* (Oxford University Press, 2021).

23   Camino Kavanagh, Madeline Carr and Nils Berglund, *Quiet Conversations: Observations from a Decade of Practice in Cyber-Related Track 1.5 and Track 2 Diplomacy*, EU Cyber Direct, November 2021, https://eucyberdirect.eu/research/quiet-conversations-observations-from-a-decade-of-practice-in-cyber-related-track-1-5-and-track-2-diplomacy.

24   US Department of State, 'A Declaration for the Future of the Internet', 28 April 2022, https://www.state.gov/declaration-for-the-future-of-the-internet.

25   UN General Assembly, 'Report of the Group of Governmental Experts on Developments in the Field of Information and Telecommunications in the Context of International Security', A/70/174, 22 July 2015, https://documents-dds-ny.un.org/doc/UNDOC/GEN/N15/228/35/PDF/N1522835.pdf.

26   UN General Assembly, 'Final Substantive Report', A/AC.290/2021/CRP.2, 10 March 2021, https://front.un-arm.org/wp-content/uploads/2021/03/Final-report-A-AC.290-2021-CRP.2.pdf.

27   US Cybersecurity and Infrastructure Security Agency, 'Alert (AA22-110A): Russian State-Sponsored and Criminal Cyber Threats to Critical Infrastructure', 20 April 2022, https://www.cisa.gov/uscert/ncas/alerts/aa22-110a.

28   Reuters, 'EU Sanctions Russian Intelligence, North Korean, Chinese Firms Over Alleged Cyberattacks', 30 July 2020, https://www.reuters.com/article/us-eu-cybercrime-russia-sanctions-idUSKCN24V32Q.

29   Matt Burgess, 'The Mystery of China's Sudden Warnings About US Hackers', *Wired*, 26 May 2022, https://www.wired.com/story/china-us-hacking-accusations/.

30   Jacquelyn G. Schneider, 'Persistent Engagement: Foundation, Evolution and Evaluation of a Strategy', *Lawfare*, 20 May 2019, https://www.lawfareblog.com/persistent-engagement-foundation-evolution-and-evaluation-strategy.

31   Vera Rusinova, 'Application of Sovereignty to Information and Communications Technologies', in Delerue and Géry (eds.), *International Law and Cybersecurity Governance* (EU Cyber Direct, July 2022), pp. 43–50, https://eucyberdirect.eu/research/international-law-and-cybersecurity-governance.

32   Russell Buchan, *Cyber Espionage and International Law* (Bloomsbury, 2021).

33   Harriet Moynihan, *The Application of International Law to State Cyberattacks: Sovereignty and Non-Intervention* (Chatham

House, December 2019), https://www.chathamhouse.org/2019/12/application-international-law-state-cyberattacks/2-application-sovereignty-cyberspace.

34   Adam Segal, 'China's Vision for Cyber Sovereignty and the Global Governance of Cyberspace', in Rolland (ed.), *An Emerging China-Centric Order: China's Vision for a New World Order in Practice* (National Bureau of Asian Research, August 2020), https://www.nbr.org/wp-content/uploads/pdfs/publications/sr87_aug2020.pdf.

35   Milton Mueller, *Will the Internet Fragment?* (Polity, 2017).

36   Jack Wagner, 'China's Cybersecurity Law: What You Need to Know', *The Diplomat*, 1 June 2017, https://thediplomat.com/2017/06/chinas-cybersecurity-law-what-you-need-to-know/.

37   James Shires, *The Politics of Cybersecurity in the Middle East* (Hurst, 2021).

38   Michael N. Schmitt (ed.), *Tallinn Manual on the International Law Applicable to Cyber Warfare* (Cambridge University Press, 2013).

39   https://www.coe.int/en/web/cybercrime/the-budapest-convention

40   Julian Ku, 'Tentative Observations on China's View on International Law and Cyber Warfare', *Lawfare*, 26 August 2017, https://www.lawfareblog.com/tentative-observations-chinas-views-international-law-and-cyber-warfare.

41   Wolff Heintschel von Heinegg, 'International Law and International Information Security: A Response to Krutskikh and Streltsov', *Tallin Paper* 9 (NATO CCD COE, 2015), https://ccdcoe.org/uploads/2018/10/TP_09_2015.pdf.

42   Summer Walker, 'The Quixotic Quest to Tackle Global Cybercrime', *Foreign Policy*, 11 February 2022, https://foreignpolicy.com/2022/02/11/un-cybercrime-treaty-russia-hacking/.

43   Luca Belli, 'Cybersecurity Convergence in the BRICS Countries', *Directions*, 17 September 2021, https://directionsblog.eu/cybersecurity-convergence-in-the-brics-countries/.

44   Duncan Hollis, 'A Brief Primer on International Law and Cyberspace', Carnegie Endowment for International Peace, 14 June 2021, https://carnegieendowment.org/2021/06/14/brief-primer-on-international-law-and-cyberspace-pub-84763.

45   Adam Segal, 'Peering Into the Future of Sino-Russian Cyber Security Cooperation', *War on the Rocks*, 10 August 2010, https://warontherocks.com/2020/08/peering-into-the-future-of-sino-russian-cyber-security-cooperation/.

46 Brad Smith, 'The Need for a Digital Geneva Convention',
    Microsoft, 14 February 2017, https://blogs.microsoft.com/on-the-
    issues/2017/02/14/need-digital-geneva-convention/.

Chapter 6

1   John Perry Barlow, 'A Declaration of the Independence of
    Cyberspace', 8 February 1996, https://www.eff.org/cyberspace-
    independence.
2   UN Development Programme, *Human Development
    Report 1994*, https://hdr.undp.org/system/files/documents//
    hdr1994encompletenostatspdf.pdf.
3   Mary Kaldor, *Human Security* (Wiley, 2007).
4   Ken Booth, *Theory of World Security* (Cambridge University Press,
    2007), p. 107.
5   Myriam Dunn Cavelty, *Cyber-Security and Threat Politics: US
    Efforts to Secure the Information Age* (Routledge, 2009).
6   Sean Lawson and Michael K. Middleton, 'Cyber Pearl Harbor:
    Analogy, Fear, and the Framing of Cyber Security Threats in the
    United States, 1991–2016', *First Monday* 24 (2019), https://doi.
    org/10.5210/fm.v24i3.9623.
7   Richard Clarke and Robert Knake, *Cyber War: The Next Threat to
    National Security and What to Do about It* (Ecco, 2012).
8   Robert M. Lee and Thomas Rid, 'OMG Cyber! Thirteen Reasons
    Why Hype Makes for Bad Policy', *The RUSI Journal* 159 (2014),
    pp. 4–12.
9   Bruce Schneier, 'Security Design: Stop Trying to Fix the User',
    Schneier on Security, 3 October 2016, https://www.schneier.com/
    blog/archives/2016/10/security_design.html.
10 Florian J. Egloff and James Shires, 'The Better Angels of Our
    Digital Nature? Offensive Cyber Capabilities and State Violence',
    European Journal of International Security (2021), https://doi.
    org/10.1017/eis.2021.20.
11 William Ralston, 'The Untold Story of a Cyberattack, a Hospital
    and a Dying Woman', *Wired*, 11 November 2020, https://www.
    wired.co.uk/article/ransomware-hospital-death-germany.
12 Ken Booth, 'Security and Emancipation', *Review of International
    Studies* 17 (1991), pp. 313–26.
13 James Shires, *The Politics of Cybersecurity in the Middle East*
    (Hurst, 2021).
14 Justin Sherman, 'How Much Cyber Sovereignty Is Too Much Cyber
    Sovereignty?', *Council on Foreign Relations*, 30 October 2019,

https://www.cfr.org/blog/how-much-cyber-sovereignty-too-much-cyber-sovereignty.

15   Fahmida Y. Rashid, 'Surveillance Is the Business Model of the Internet: Bruce Schneier', 29 April 2014, *Security Week*, https://www.securityweek.com/surveillance-business-model-internet-bruce-schneier.

16   Shoshana Zuboff, *The Age of Surveillance Capitalism: The Fight for a Human Future at the Frontier of Power* (Profile Books, 2019).

17   Daniel Moore, *Offensive Cyber Operations: Understanding Intangible Warfare* (Hurst, 2022).

18   John Arquilla, *Bitskrieg: The New Challenge of Cyberwarfare* (Polity, 2021).

19   Ryan Jenkins, 'Cyberwarfare as Ideal War', in Allhoff, Henschke and Strawser (eds.), *Binary Bullets: The Ethics of Cyberwarfare* (Oxford University Press, 2016), pp. 89–114.

20   George Lucas, *Ethics and Cyber Warfare: The Quest for Responsible Security in the Age of Digital Warfare* (Oxford University Press, 2017).

21   Max Smeets, 'A US History of Not Conducting Cyber Attacks', *Bulletin of the Atomic Scientists* 78 (2022), pp. 208–13, https://doi.org/10.1080/00963402.2022.2087380.

22   Joe Devanny, 'The Ethics of Offensive Cyber Operations', *Foreign Policy Centre*, 3 December 2020, https://fpc.org.uk/the-ethics-of-offensive-cyber-operations/.

Chapter 7

1   Ronald J. Deibert, *Reset: Reclaiming the Internet for Civil Society* (Anansi, 2020), p. 34.

FURTHER READING

Assuming you stuck with this book to the end, where might you go next to learn more about cybersecurity? How might you join the conversation I alluded to at the end? There is no substitute for doing your own research into a given topic and cybersecurity is no exception. I have provided some suggestions for further reading below, each of which is an accessible non-technical introduction to key aspects of cybersecurity. Following the footnotes in these books will lead to a vast resource of academic and non-academic publications on all aspects of cybersecurity, including the invaluable work of think tanks and other research organizations. Academic publications are often hidden behind paywalls, but much can be found in draft form via search tools like Google Scholar.

Despite their excellence, few published works capture the unfolding diversity of cybersecurity or the pace at which the digital environment evolves. Fortunately, most major newspapers and current affairs magazines regularly carry cybersecurity stories, as do the broadcast networks. Often, these are framed as 'cyberwar' or use other militarized or hyperbolic language, so discretion is advised. Nevertheless, they serve an important purpose in raising awareness of cybersecurity issues and many are crucial sources of evidence and insight about what cybersecurity looks like in real time. So too is a plethora of specialist online publications, blogs and social media accounts, some of which are referenced in the notes to this book.

Awareness is one thing, but engagement is another. Paying attention to what our elected representatives and diplomats say and do is essential for keeping abreast of the political dimensions of cybersecurity. At present, there is a somewhat underdeveloped public conversation around cybersecurity policy and strategy and most of it attends to its more glamorous military and intelligence dimensions. These are important, for sure, but we also need to think about the longer-term implications of digital transformation and the role of cybersecurity in pursuing social, economic and political benefits for individuals and society. Civil society groups like The Citizen Lab in Canada and the Berkman Center for Internet and Society in the US are essential sources on cybersecurity and related issues and there are many others too. Cybersecurity requires a diversity of voices and inputs to develop responses to cybersecurity issues that are appropriate, proportionate and serve social interests, as well as those of corporations and high politics – perhaps your voice can be one of them.

John Arquilla, *Bitskrieg: The New Challenge of Cyberwarfare* (Polity Press, 2021)

Ben Buchanan, *The Hacker and the State: Cyber Attacks and the New Normal of Geopolitics* (Harvard University Press, 2020)

Ronald J. Deibert, *Reset: Reclaiming the Internet for Civil Society* (Anansi Press, 2020)

Laura DeNardis, *The Internet in Everything: Freedom and Security in a World with No Off Switch* (Yale University Press, 2020)

Alexander Klimburg, *The Darkening Web: The War for Cyberspace* (Penguin, 2017)

Kieron O'Hara and Wendy Hall, *Four Internets: Data, Geopolitics, and the Governance of Cyberspace* (Oxford University Press, 2021)

Nicole Perlroth, *This Is How They Tell Me the World Ends: The Cyber Weapons Arms Race* (Bloomsbury, 2021)

Damien van Puyvelde and Aaron F. Brantly, *Cybersecurity: Politics, Governance and Conflict in Cyberspace* (Polity Press, 2019)

Bruce Schneier, *Click Here to Kill Everybody: Security and Survival in a Hyper-Connected World* (W.W. Norton, 2018)

Adam Segal, *The Hacked World Order: How Nations Fight, Trade, Maneuver, and Manipulate in the Digital Age* (PublicAffairs, 2016)

Brad Smith, *Tools and Weapons: The Promise and the Peril of the Digital Age* (Penguin, 2019)

Kim Zetter, *Countdown to Zero Day: Stuxnet and the Launch of the World's First Digital Weapon* (Crown, 2014)

INDEX

Page numbers in *italics* refer to illustrations